GREY SPACES

GREY SPACES

Searching Out the Church in the Shadows of Abuse

Jeffrey W. Driver

CASCADE *Books* • Eugene, Oregon

GREY SPACES
SEARCHING OUT THE CHURCH IN THE SHADOWS OF ABUSE

Copyright © 2022 Jeffrey W. Driver. All rights reserved. Except for brief quotations in critical publications or reviews, no part of this book may be reproduced in any manner without prior written permission from the publisher. Write: Permissions, Wipf and Stock Publishers, 199 W. 8th Ave., Suite 3, Eugene, OR 97401.

Cascade Books
An Imprint of Wipf and Stock Publishers
199 W. 8th Ave., Suite 3
Eugene, OR 97401

www.wipfandstock.com

PAPERBACK ISBN: 978-1-6667-3616-8
HARDCOVER ISBN: 978-1-6667-9414-4
EBOOK ISBN: 978-1-6667-9415-1

Cataloguing-in-Publication data:

Names: Driver, Jeffrey W., author.

Title: Grey spaces : searching out the church in the shadows of abuse / Jeffrey W. Driver.

Description: Eugene, OR: Cascade Books, 2022 | Includes bibliographical references and index.

Identifiers: ISBN 978-1-6667-3616-8 (paperback) | ISBN 978-1-6667-9414-4 (hardcover) | ISBN 978-1-6667-9415-1 (ebook)

Subjects: LCSH: Church—Authority. | Church controversies. | Social institutions.

Classification: BT738 D71 2022 (paperback) | BT738 (ebook)

VERSION NUMBER 110422

New Revised Standard Version Bible, copyright 2989, Division of Christian Education of the National Council of the Churches of Christian the United States of America. Used by permission. All rights reserved.

CONTENTS

A Note on Richard Hooker's Lawes of Ecclesiastical Polity | vii

Acknowledgments | ix

Chapter 1
The Odium of Institutions | 1

Chapter 2
"Over the Institutional Church"? | 12

Chapter 3
Dominion, Distortion, and Domination | 28

Chapter 4
Institutions: Dwelling in the Grey Spaces | 51

Chapter 5
The Power of Symbols—the Symbols of Power | 73

Chapter 6
Clericalism: Playing the Insider Game | 97

Chapter 7
Moses, Management, Bishops, Budgets, and Busyness | 114

Chapter 8
Searching Out the Church in the Shadows of Shame | 128

An Afterword: The Emmaus Road to Recognition | 136

Bibliography | 141
Index | 151

A NOTE ON RICHARD HOOKER'S
LAWES OF ECCLESIASTICAL POLITY

I HAVE MOST FREQUENTLY cited the Folger Library Edition of *The Works of Richard Hooker* (ed. W. Speed Hill), with the abbreviation *FLE*. Footnotes are set out as follow: Book number. chapter: verse; Folger Library volume number, page number. Where I have included larger quotations I have tended to include more contemporary translations in the interest of accessibility. In these instances I have usually also included the Folger Library Edition details.

ACKNOWLEDGMENTS

IN THE MIDST OF a diocesan crisis caused by the revelation of widespread historic sexual abuse of children, it is almost impossible to step back and reflect deeply about underlying influences. The first priority must be to develop a pastoral response to the survivors, and then to put in place more rigorous measures for child protection and better education and screening of leaders.

During the early years of my episcopate in the Anglican Diocese of Adelaide (2005–2016), the immediacy of crisis occupied much of my time and emotional energy, as well as that of the diocese as a whole. We were a community processing grief. During the latter few years that I was in Adelaide, the requirements of the Royal Commission into Institutional Responses to Child Sexual Abuse once more absorbed much of the time and energies of the diocesan leadership and also rekindled a sense of grief and shame within the diocesan community. Staff needed ongoing support and professional debriefing, which the diocese provided.

There is never enough that can be done to respond to the tragedy of abuse. There is never enough sorrow to express in recognition of the trauma of those who were abused, particularly when that abuse occurred in a relationship of sacred trust. But I want to acknowledge a group of people in the Diocese of Adelaide, who with good heart, gave deeply of themselves. In the grey-grief, there were moments of deep humanity. Sometimes that humanity came in the face of survivors of abuse who showed more grace to the church than the church had shown to them.

In all the busyness of the immediate, the questions niggled: "How could the church I had sought to serve for all these years allow things to develop to this extent? Were we that naïve, or blind? Or was it plain denial?" In 2017 the Royal Commission into Institutional Responses to Child Sexual Abuse brought down its *Final Report*. The product of years of work

ACKNOWLEDGMENTS

included fifty-seven public hearings, and more than eight thousand private sessions. The royal commission formally put to the churches some of the questions that had been niggling at me. The *Final Report* acknowledged that the churches had taken some important steps in putting in place processes to respond to survivors, as well as enhanced child protection. But it challenged the churches to look deeper; to reflect on the theological and cultural factors that predisposed the possibility of abuse and the defensive responses that tended to follow, at least initially.

Since retiring from the Diocese of Adelaide, I have continued to wrestle with these questions and this little book is one product of that wrestling. To the extent that it offers some small wisdom, it is as Helen Reddy put it, "wisdom born of pain";[1] a sense of not being able to do enough, the grief of sometimes well-intended failing, as well as deep appreciation of the gifts of others as we struggled together. If the Diocese of Adelaide was in a better place when I left in 2016 is a tribute to the wonderful people of that diocese.

What follows in this small volume is not an attempt at easy answers. Rather it is a hopeful encouragement to further reflection, recognizing that institutions, being what they are, will tend to deal with problems only sufficiently to make them "go away," then move on. The church should not be like that.

Most of this small volume was written during the COVID-19 pandemic, which, along with many far more serious effects, made the conversations that are at the heart of any writing endeavor much more difficult. There are a range of conversation partners that I must acknowledge: Bruce Kaye and Stephen Pickard, from Charles Sturt University Australia; Martyn Percy, from Christ Church Oxford; John Wright, previously dean of St John's Auckland; Muriel Porter; and finally the late Gary Bouma, who in the last months of his life enlarged my limited sociological perspectives and did so with patience and humor. My local parish, St Peter's by the Lake, Paynesville, keeps me encouraged and grounded. And there is my wife, Lindy, who has a gift of forbearance. To the team at Wipf and Stock, I once again express my thanks for the opportunity to publish, as well as their patience and guidance along the way. Whatever insights are brought together here come from many; whatever shortcomings are entirely my own.

In what passes for retirement, I have been deeply involved with Newton College, Popondetta, the Anglican Church of Papua New Guinea's one college for the formation of clergy. I left there on March 21, 2021, the day

---

1. Helen Reddy, *I Am Woman*, 1971.

ACKNOWLEDGMENTS

before flights were shut down because of the pandemic. The students at Newton College live in confronting need, with little assistance for college fees, let alone basic living expenses. They have a bare subsistence lifestyle. As they do their theology, they have to make the sort of choices that those of us in the privileged West struggle to understand: "Can I buy a little rice and soap, or must I take my child to the doctor? Can I put up with my own heath condition just a little longer, so I can pay the school fees for my children?" Their lives have been made all the more precarious by the pandemic. Writing this book in the comfort and safety of my home in Australia, I think of them and long to return.

Chapter 1

THE ODIUM OF INSTITUTIONS

AUSTRALIANS HAVE A PARTICULAR use of the idiom "on the nose." Whereas in many countries, this colloquial phrase means "accurate" or "precise" (thus a precise estimate or answer might be described as "right on the nose"), in Australia such a description can be far from complimentary. It suggests something is distasteful or unpleasant; it stinks. For many Australians, the institutional church is "on the nose."

Throughout the Western world, institutions are experiencing a loss of confidence and even antipathy, and these attitudes have extended to the churches.[1] Sadly, there have often been good reasons for the public disdain.

---

1. Heclo, *On Thinking Institutionally*, 46–79.
Here I am using the term "institution" in a wider sense than in some definitions offered, largely because I am trying to reflect popular usage and also to align with the language of the Australian *Royal Commission into Institutional Responses to Child Sexual Abuse*, which will be referred to from time to time. At the same time, it is important to recognize that there is an ongoing debate about the difference between "institutions" and "organizations" and we will refer to that debate further as we go along. Hugh Heclo comments: "Unfortunately, as far as definitions go, reviews of the scholarly literature on institutions are an invitation to frustration. The reviewers generally make a point of describing how the leading experts on the subject simply cannot agree on what constitutes an institution." By way of offering a tentative working definition for the purposes of this book, we might think of an institution as a chronologically durable social structure or construct that influences or constrains human behavior as well as enabling pursuit of a shared and greater good. An organization, on the other hand, can be seen as an organized group of people brought together to achieve a common purpose or objective.
See also Smith, *Institutional Intelligence*, 4–5. For a slightly narrower definition of institutions, see North, *Institutions*, 4–5.

In recent decades a succession of leading institutions around the world have been exposed as self-serving, acting in ways that conflict with their founding narrative and against the better interests of the wider public. Too many institutional leaders have been found to be self-interested and willing to turn a blind eye to dubious and corrupt practices in the organizations they lead.

In the Australian context, major institutional failures have been highlighted by a series of royal commissions and public inquiries. Sectors that have had corrupt, abusive, or self-serving behavior exposed through these public mechanisms include the banks, defence force, trade unions, the judiciary, aged care institutions, and the churches.[2] For the churches, it was the *Royal Commission into Institutional Responses to Child Sexual Abuse* that delivered a scathing assessment of the church's lack of protective care for the vulnerable, both as children and as traumatized adults.[3]

The royal commission was announced by the then-prime minister Julia Gillard in 2012.[4] Public hearings began in 2013 and the deliberations of the commission concluded with the publication of a final report in December 2017. The work of the commission included fifty-seven public hearings, more than eight thousand private sessions, and some 2,500 referrals to the authorities. The commission's *Final Report* acknowledged that failures in providing care and safety for children were not confined to religious institutions, but went on to say that the failures in religious institutions were "particularly troubling" since these same entities had been "among the most respected institutions in our society." Much of the media attention related to the royal commission was focused on the major churches and this was supported by confronting statistics; the commission heard about more than 4,500 instances of abuse in religious institutions, and of these about 2,500 were in Roman Catholic institutions and about one thousand were in Anglican institutions.[5]

The commission introduced its final report under the title "A National Tragedy." While recognizing that many of the churches had put in place

2. Commonwealth of Australia, Royal Commission Final Report, 5.

3. In Australia there was on average a gap of more than twenty years between an incident of child sexual abuse and its subsequent reporting.

4. The Australian *Royal Commission into Institutional Responses to Child Sexual Abuse* (2012–2017) was the longest, largest, and highest funded public inquiry into historical institutional child sexual abuse in Australian history.

5. An important factor was the number of residential institutions and schools operated by these two denominations.

enhanced child protection measures and had developed redress schemes for survivors, the Final Report challenged the churches to look at underlying theological and cultural factors that predisposed the churches to respond poorly to their responsibilities for the protection of children.

The challenge from the royal commission for the churches to reflect deeply on those theological and cultural factors that predisposed the possibility of abuse, then the defensive responses that followed, provide the impetus for this book. These explorations will be pursued beyond the tragedy of child abuse into a wider space of dialogue about how the church expresses its life institutionally and how those institutional expressions reflect, or might better reflect, the gospel of Christ in a world that is increasingly skeptical about institutions.

This chapter will consider the specific concerns raised by the royal commission within a brief survey of broader attitudes towards institutions in Western societies. Chapter 2 will examine the nature of the church in institutional expression. It will engage with suggestions that the institutionalizing of faith is at odds with the church's call to be a community (*koinonia*) of believers. While arguing that the church cannot escape the institutional in the world around it, and that it cannot persevere in the world without some institutional expression, we will explore the distinction that Avery Dulles makes between the necessity of institutional expression and what he calls institutionalization, with the latter referring to a tendency to make the institutional dominant in the church's self-understanding and producing a clericalist and hierarchical expression where power almost always flows from top to bottom.

Chapters 3 and 4 will explore the tensions of power within institutionality, surveying these themes through the story of the people of God. All institutional expressions within the people of God are adapted from the world of their time. Necessary, even providential, though they might be, they are human, frail, and always carry the possibility of distorting the distinctive nature and call of God's people. Institutions always have a shadow side. Health is found neither in retreating into a spiritual ideal, nor surrendering to "the powers that be," but in living honestly within the uncomfortable grey space of tension between the two.

Chapter 5 will look at how symbol and ritual give unspoken expression to a cosmology of power that sometimes powerfully contradicts the church's developing narrative. Humans are symbol makers, so a simplistic abandoning of the symbolic is usually an invitation for a new complex of symbols to arise, often with no less risk of distortion. An alternative is to look at how symbols might be "re-placed" (placed differently), "re-framed" (given a different contextual framework) and "re-received" (as expressions of living tradition).

Chapters 6 and 7 will explore structures and leadership and how they impact on the disposition of power. We will look at clericalism and how notions such as the indelibility of orders can be used to support it, creating an ecclesial caste system that reduces accountability and distorts the very nature of ordained vocation. In these chapters we will also look at the church's institutional structures, with a particular focus on the structures of traditional churches such as those of the Anglican Communion—the diocese and the office of the bishop.

This book does not seek to provide a ready recipe for change. To attempt to do that would be to deny the complexity and particularity that is always part of the life of the church, as it is also an inevitable part of cultural change. Chapter 8 will propose some directions for wider discussion and identify some signs of hope among the shadows of shame created by the failure to protect vulnerable people who were abused in what should have been a relationship of sacred trust, often because the protection of the institution was put first.

Deeper currents

As with many other major institutions in Western society over the same time period, it may be said of the churches that they gained community distrust the "old-fashioned way"—by earning it.[6] The exposure of governance and leadership failures across a range of major institutions may have provided the presenting cause for disillusionment, but there are other more indirect influences in Western society that should not be overlooked. Heclo suggests that to fully understand the prevailing widespread cynicism about institutions, we need understand the effect not just of what he calls "performance based distrust," but also "culture based distrust."[7] While recognizing the complexity of modern society, Heclo argues that there is in the West a prevailing cultural norm that each individual "has the right to live as he or she pleases so long as we do not interfere with the right of other people to do likewise." This emphasis on the rights of the individual, he suggests, has

6. Heclo, *On Thinking Institutionally*, 15.
7. Heclo, *On Thinking Institutionally*, 32.

replaced an earlier social compact in which the self-realization of the individual was more deeply linked to a shared pursuit of the common good, and in which the choice to subordinate self to the social good was not seen as being at odds with the ideal of personal fulfillment.[8]

Here we can offer little more than a passing acknowledgement of the complex and interrelated currents that have produced this shift in Western consciousness. Even to name the powerful streams of the Enlightenment, Romanticism, and Modernism without significant qualification is to take the risk of oversimplification. Each of these movements was complex, multifaceted, and capable of different expression in different places, influenced by different events. The gifts of the Enlightenment are undoubted and multiple: freedom for unfettered inquiry, the affirmation of human rights, respect for the individual, and the cultivation of tolerance. Yet, as Heclo points out, the Enlightenment's almost unlimited confidence in the power of human reason also tended to denigrate the habits and institutional loyalties of ordinary life: "Anything engrained in institutions were simply an impediment to the freedom of individuals and societies to create their desired future."[9]

Romanticism balanced the Enlightenment emphasis on reason with its focus on self-expression and creative imagination, but it also made its own contribution to eroding the place of institutions in human society. The fixed givenness of institutions and their assumption of authority was seen as a denial of Romanticism's stress on individual freedom and creativity.[10] Modernity came as another wave, rejecting much of the Western humanist past and looking to create a new world and a new humanity through science, industry, and technology. The twentieth century was to be the first in which humans "freed themselves from the past and its interdictions."[11] The horrors of two world wars reinforced the modernist conviction that humanity had been failed by incompetent and merciless social institutions that deserved to be abandoned.

---

8. Heclo, *On Thinking Institutionally*, 35. Heclo quotes polling expert Daniel Yankelovich: "Americans now believe the old giving/getting compact needlessly restricts the individual, while advancing the power of large institutions—government and business particularly—who use the power to enhance their own interest at the expense of the public."

9. Heclo, *On Thinking Institutionally*, 178.

10. Heclo, *On Thinking Institutionally*, 179.

11. Conrad, *Modern Times, Modern Places*, 13.

Since then the incessant message from modern literature and the arts has been that institutions are not something to which authentic, free, and savvy individuals should want to be attached. There is a phony and diabolical "churchiness" about them. They crush the individual's aesthetic aspiration for life. Their moral standards are likely to be incompatible with personal fulfilment.[12]

Heclo argues that the institution-aversion of Western society is also reinforced by associated political and economic systems, even though they themselves are arguably institutional. The modern market, he suggests, has become a "vast machine for selling the common man [sic] on the idea that he and his immediate wants are the principal thing" and "constantly teaches a short-term, self-centred ethic of personal gratification. This view is incessantly marketed as the standard by which to judge what is personally fulfilling, thus working against institutional thinking . . ."[13]

Many aspects of modern political democracy support these traits of the economic system. For all its great strengths, democracy has at its heart not the subordination of the individual self to a shared good, but to giving a political and societal expression to the philosophical primacy of the individual. To state the obvious, in a democratic system, what rules supreme is the individual's preference expressed at the ballot box. The democratic system also tends to shorten time horizons; an election-winning government has come to power only through conquering what was there before. In politics, the past is a dead hand. At the same time, its vision of the future tends to be blurred beyond the date of the next election, or even the immediacy of the twenty-four-hour news cycle. Thus, the sense of the long-term—something that is intrinsic to institutional life—is discounted by modern democracy's limited horizons.[14]

So while many institutions in recent times have provided their own performance-based reasons justifying community suspicion and skepticism, and as appalling as some of the particular instances have been, they are carried along by a deeper, powerful current in Western society and that prevailing current is institution-averse. To return to that less-than-complimentary phrase from the Australian colloquial, in the twenty-first-century West, institutions tend to be "on the nose."

---

12. Heclo, *On Thinking Institutionally*, 180.
13. Heclo, *On Thinking Institutionally*, 167.
14. Heclo, *On Thinking Institutionally*, 163–84.

But not always

As in most countries, Australian cities experienced prolonged COVID-19 lockdowns during 2020 and into 2021. Naturally, throughout this time, news reporting was dominated by updates on the pandemic and responses to it. For some of this lockdown period in Australia, however, coverage about COVID-19 was often closely followed in news bulletins by an update on an appeal by an Australian Roman Catholic cardinal, George Pell, against a conviction for child sexual abuse.[15]

As the cardinal's trial and subsequent appeal continued, multicolored ribbons were often strung along fences or tied to other fixtures outside churches and cathedrals where he had served as a priest, bishop, and archbishop. "Loud fences," as they are called, have become an international symbol of disdain for the response of the churches to the tragedy of child sexual abuse, and more broadly an expression of public skepticism and disengagement with the church as an institution.

During the same lockdown period in Australia, there were other public displays that provided a visual contrast. In a Melbourne bayside suburb a large figure emerged on a building. It was of a health care worker in an Atlas pose, in blue scrubs and with large spread angel wings, holding a massive globe on his shoulders.[16] Images with a similar theme appeared throughout the country, along with scribbled thanks in shop windows, paying tribute and offering thanks to those who worked in health and aged care institutions and services, putting themselves at risk to protect others from a global pandemic. Again, these public displays and expressions had their parallels around the globe.

Institution-wary twenty-first-century Australians, like members of the public in many countries, were quick to honor the contribution of frontline institutions and the people within them who selflessly protected communities through a year of threat and crisis. Clearly not all institutions are "on the nose"—at least not all of the time.[17]

---

15. Cardinal Pell's conviction was subsequently overturned on appeal in the High Court.

16. The mural was painted by Brigitte Dawson and Melissa Turner in the Melbourne beachside suburb of Black Rock.

17. Just weeks before the outbreak of COVID-19 gripped the world's attention, much of eastern Australia was ravaged by immense bushfires, bringing death, destruction, and apocalyptic darkness. Images of firefighters and defence force personnel battling these hellish conditions were seen around the globe. Street art at the time included pointed

Exceptions that prove?

Many people in any number of Western countries today may well regard it as obvious that institutions should be regarded with distrust. Without much hesitation members of the public will probably be able to list powerful, prestigious, and previously trusted institutions that have given themselves a bad name as scandalous or corrupt behavior has been exposed. The same people may well be less aware of the complex and powerful intellectual currents that have also influenced their conclusions, but the result is the same: the prevailing twenty-first-century attitude towards institutions is one of skepticism and distrust.

Yet, as we have noted, where an institution and those serving within it are seen to be acting selflessly and with a commitment to the common good, then the inclination to suspicion can be suspended and honor given. Given the prevailing disposition, the bar of approval is often set high, as the risk and danger experienced by healthcare professionals during the COVID-19 pandemic illustrated.[18] The question can nevertheless be asked, what rule or rules do these exceptions prove? Can we account for the healthiness of some institutions and the public esteem accorded them entirely as relating to the exemplary performance of individuals within them and the lack of scandal surrounding them? Inversely, is it enough to attribute the disdain that has been accorded to some institutions to the behavior of some "bad apples" within them, along with the system failures that allowed them to get away with their bad behavior?

In regard to abusive behavior against vulnerable minors, no consideration of contributing factors or underlying influences can be used to minimize or reduce responsibility for what was done. However, the Australian *Royal Commission into Institutional Responses to Child Sexual Abuse* did encourage the churches to looker deeper and to consider underlying causes

---

criticism of politicians for responding too slowly to the crisis or for doing too little about climate change, but there were many artistic expressions honoring the fire services for their heroic work. Among the many murals for which Hosier Lane in Melbourne is famous, there was one of a firefighting koala by artist Andrew Gibbons. The only words were, "Thank you RFS" (Rural Fire Service). While the various fire services might more properly be regarded as organizations than institutions, there were many other bodies involved, including the Australian Defence Force and Police. The churches and other faith communities provided hundreds of volunteer support workers.

18. Similarly the willingness of Salvation Army workers during World War II to offer care while exposing themselves to considerable risk left a legacy of good will that lasted for decades.

and influences that included "a combination of cultural, governance and theological factors," contributing to the vulnerability of children to abuse and "the likelihood of religious institutions responding poorly when abuse occurs."[19]

Referring to the Anglican Church, the commission identified an "internal culture" and "underlying theological and scriptural beliefs and practices" as contributing to the vulnerability of children to abuse and "the likelihood of religious institutions responding poorly when abuse occurs."[20] A similar comment is made about the Roman Catholic Church:

> Child sexual abuse by Catholic clergy and religious may be explained by a combination of psychosexual and other related factors on the part of the individual perpetrator, and a range of institutional factors, including theological, governance and cultural factors. The same theological, governance and cultural factors that contributed to the occurrence of abuse also contributed to the inadequate responses of Catholic institutions to that abuse.[21]

Among the central factors identified by the royal commission as "underpinning and linked to all other factors" was a culture of clericalism, springing from the status of people in religious ministry.

> In several of the religious institutions we examined, the central factor, underpinning and linked to all other factors, was the status of people in religious ministry. We repeatedly heard that the status of people in religious ministry, described in some contexts as clericalism, contributed to the occurrence of child sexual abuse in religious institutions, as well as to inadequate institutional responses.[22]

The first response of an institution to crisis is usually, and often necessarily, programmatic and structural. As many of the submissions to the Australian royal commission detailed, from the late 1990s and particularly through the first decade of the twenty-first century, most of the churches implemented a range of structural, educational, and disciplinary responses to the emerging picture of the historic abuse of minors. These responses were recognized by the royal commission in its final report, which at the

---

19. Commonwealth of Australia, Royal Commission Final Report, 28.
20. Commonwealth of Australia, Royal Commission Final Report, 28.
21. Commonwealth of Australia, Royal Commission Final Report, 42.
22. Commonwealth of Australia, Royal Commission Final Report, 28.

same time flagged important areas where further changes were still required, the most challenging being to address the underlying and contributing aspects of institutional culture.[23]

If we think of culture as the underlying beliefs, values, assumptions, habits, and ways of interacting that are deeply embedded and often unconsciously assumed within institutions, then it becomes obvious that cultural change is as difficult as it is essential. As Edgar Schein points out, "organizational learning, development, and planned change cannot be understood without considering culture as a primary source of resistance to change."[24]

Because organizational culture generates meaning, values, identity, and security, the consideration of institutional culture within the church takes us necessarily into the realms of ecclesiology. Although from time to time we will touch on insights from the social sciences, in the end, the focus and aspiration here is ecclesiological—in focusing on institutional culture, to allow the gospel to speak into the life of the church once more.

This is a place of *metanoia*. Often translated as "repentance" and understood as a turning away from sin, the word means more than this. It has the sense of a profound reorientation, or change of worldview. Beyond necessary expressions of apology and sorrow, and beyond the necessary programmatic or structural changes, this takes us to the deeper questions of church as *being*.

As the church seeks to address its institutional culture, including the dysfunctional elements painfully highlighted in recent times, it is challenged once more by its high calling and at the same time confronted by what Hans Küng called the "dark shadow" aspects of its being that will always be a part of its historical expression. Ecclesiology, argued Küng, must take into consideration the shadow nature of the church if it is to avoid

---

23. As of the end of 2020, not all relevant organizations had signed up to a national redress scheme established under the Australian Federal Government. And even within some of the churches there is the possibility of great disparity in processes and outcomes. For instance, the royal commission highlighted the governance of the Anglican Church of Australia, in which each of the twenty-three dioceses have a high degree of autonomy, as inhibiting the development of uniform measures for child protection and redress across that church. The Anglican Church in Australia still lacks the commonality of approach that the royal commission flagged as desirable, although greater commonality has been achieved at a provincial (state-by-state) level.

24. Schein, *Organizational Culture*, xiv. To take some liberties with an anecdote possibly attributed erroneously to Peter Drucker: culture eats strategy for breakfast, organizational programs for lunch, and structures for dessert.

dangerous abstraction and idealism, and take as its starting point the message of the gospel.[25]

---

25. Küng, *Church*, 28–29.

Chapter 2

"OVER THE INSTITUTIONAL CHURCH"?

IN A SLIGHTLY JADED moment, a retiring bishop friend reflected that he was "over the institutional church." He had spent years battling institutional decline and problems in several diocesan agencies that threatened the very life of a small country diocese, so his frustration that institutional demands had overwhelmed other aspects of his ministry was understandable. In all likelihood that frustration at the constant institutional drain on his time and energy was also preventing him from seeing some of the many other good things that he had done and would leave behind as he retired.

My own journey towards involvement in the Anglican Church as a young man was marked by a different sort of leeriness about the institutional. Growing from my teens to my twenties, through the late 1960s into the 1970s, I was part of a generation quick to reject anything that smacked of tradition. With all the certainty so often characteristic of the young, I dismissed much of what was happening in my local parish as so much institutional repetition and made my journey though house groups, charismatic gatherings in which I was never very comfortable, and even tried the then-fashionable experiment of living "in community." There were some wonderful moments and others where personality conflicts, leadership ego and instability, as well as a lack of boundaries put the personal well-being of people at risk. The patience and grace of two or three clergy I came to know drew me back into the Anglican Church, then into its ordained ministry.

My friend's frustrated comment towards the end of his ministry, and my own somewhat less humble assumptions at the beginning of mine, pose an important question, and that is whether or not the church is necessarily institutional. To put it another way, if my friend is "over" the institutional church, is there any other sort of church?

There have been some theological heavyweights who have supported the view that in its essence, the church is not and should not be at all institutional, that the development of institutional forms in the church was a distortion and a loss. The eminent Swiss theologian Emil Brunner (1889–1966) maintained that institutional Christianity was a substitute for "banished *pnuema*" (spirit). The apostolic *ecclesia*, argued Brunner, was fundamentally and foundationally a fellowship, "the sphere of actual and realised fellowship with Christ" where Christ was truly "embodied." This early *koinonia* was of a different character than that which later emerged in the institutional church. While recognizing that the organizational shifts in the church were a result of numerical expansion and in response to the threats of heresy, Brunner identified a theological shift in moving from *ecclesia* to institution, relating it to a growing sacramental understanding of salvation, and associated with that, the need for a sacred priesthood and inevitable hierarchy.[1] "The community of Jesus Christ is henceforth identical with an organization, an institution, a holy thing."[2]

Writing a little later, the equally influential Jürgen Moltmann argued that the growth of the church as an institution with hierarchical structures was a "false development" that led to a "quenching of the Spirit and was an impediment to the charismatic church."[3]

Both Brunner and Moltmann tended to equate the institutional with an uneven, or hierarchical, distribution of power within human sociality. In this they are probably right. As we shall see, the social sciences tell us that one of the major functions of human institutions is the distribution of power, and that this distribution will, in varying degrees, inevitably turn out to be marked by differentials. What the social sciences also tell us, however, is that institutions are a necessary and unavoidable part of human life. We are left with a paradox. Without institutions human community cannot continue, but at the same time, as Brunner and Moltmann were concerned to point out, institutions can diminish or take away community. This brings us back to the comment by my friend about being "over the institutional

---

1. Brunner, *Misunderstanding of the Church*, 46–79.
2. Brunner, *Misunderstanding of the Church*, 84–96.
3. Moltmann, *Church in the Power of the Spirit*, 305.

church," and to that important ecclesiological rejoinder; is there any other kind of church?

Can't live without them, struggle to live with them

Institutions are about people living together with some stability over time. In any sustained human grouping, patterns of relating and behaving will inevitably emerge if chaos is to be avoided, needs are to be met, and the viability of life sustained. Imagine a sampling of human beings from planet Earth, plucked from various continents by some alien means, and deposited on a strangely familiar exoplanet thousands of light years away. The environment is suitable, but if they are to survive they will quickly have to organize. They will need to attend to the immediate tasks of creating shelter, gathering food, finding water, and protecting themselves. They may not all speak the same language, so they will have to quickly sort out some basic means of communication, signs, and signaling. As time goes on it will become evident that some are better at gathering and some are better at growing. Specialization will occur so that everyone gets just a little more, but then they will have to find a way to distribute goods amongst themselves: "so much of this is worth so much of that." That bartering will inevitably develop into settled conventions. As a group they will probably need to meet from time to time to settle disputes and solve problems, and they will have to sort out an agreed way to have these meetings. Leadership will emerge and then some settled ways of choosing leaders will follow. With this sort of organization there is every chance many of them will live long lives on their new exoplanet home. If life is to continue and even flourish past that first generation of exoplanet settlers, however, much of that organization, learning, and experience as to what is helpful and what is not, what is to be valued and what is not, will need to be passed on. Enter the institution.

Scholars continue to debate about the best definition of an institution.[4] The following complexity of words from Jonathan Turner is fairly typical:

---

4. Heclo, *On Thinking Institutionally*, 46–79. As noted earlier, Heclo comments: "Unfortunately, as far as definitions go, reviews of the scholarly literature on institutions are an invitation to frustration. The reviewers generally make a point of describing how the leading experts on the subject simply cannot agree on what constitutes an institution" (46). An organization can be seen as an organized group of people brought together to achieve a common purpose or achieve objectives.

a complex of positions, roles, norms and values lodged in particular types of social structures and organising relatively stable patterns of human activity with respect to fundamental problems in producing life-sustaining resources, in reproducing individuals, and in sustaining viable societal structures within a given environment.[5]

Beyond the technicalities of definitional debates, there are some characteristics of institutions about which most agree. Institutions have a long "shelf life." Whereas an organization might be seen as a group of people working towards a specific and time-limited task or goal, institutions will generally reproduce themselves well beyond the founding group and will have ongoing functions. Institutions are like a compass. They help locate people in their social interactions and provide guidance for the way; or to put it more formally, they are capable of influencing or constraining human behavior. Institutions act like a filter. They reduce the anxiety and complexity of endless choices by simplifying and mediating the world through established values and modes of behavior.[6] Institutions also provide a social story. Part of the durability of institutions is that they tend to have supporting myths, narratives, and symbols, which provide a sense of identity.

Institutions might take different forms in different societies, but all societies tend to have institutions related to the fundamentals of humans living together: determining kinship and relationships, legitimizing and regulating the use of power, enabling the distribution of wealth, transmitting knowledge, and providing for access to greater meaning or a sense of the transcendent.[7] Institutions are essential building blocks of human society and so there is no escaping them in the church.

The church is impacted upon and influenced by external institutions every day. From great matters of law to the minutiae of building codes; from the weighty matters of child protection down to local government regulations as to the proper labeling of a sponge cake for a fundraising stall. Not only can the church not escape the institutional nature of the world around it, most of the time it enjoys the benefits that flow from social institutions

---

5. Turner, *Institutional Order*, 6.

6. Luhmann, *Trust and Power*, 17–18.

7. See "Social Institutions" in https://www.sociologyguide.com/basic-concepts/Social-Institutions.php. For a more detailed discussion, consult Berger and Luckmann, *Social Construction of Reality*, 70–96.

in the form of order, stability, predictability, and the means to communicate and share resources.

The church cannot escape the institutional workings of the world around it, but does it need to be an institution itself? There are two levels at which we might answer this question. The first is at a pragmatic level and it brings us back to those characteristics of institutions described above. If the church sees itself as an organization that aspires to endure over time, then some form of institutional expression is necessary. If it sees itself as passing on a story, or nurturing values, or having a role in education, then it cannot avoid developing institutional forms, because human society does most of these things through institutions. If the church was ever to be more than an ephemeral blossoming it could not avoid the practical reality of developing institutional forms.

The second level of exploring the question as to whether the church needs to be an institution takes us beyond the purely practical into the theological, to take some account of the church's own understanding of its place and role in the world. Shelves of books are written around this subject more generally, but if we are to confine ourselves to the question as to whether the church *needs* institutional expression, then an appropriate starting place is the Great Commission:

> And Jesus came and said to them, "All authority in heaven and on earth has been given to me. Go therefore and make disciples of all nations, baptizing them in the name of the Father and of the Son and of the Holy Spirit and teaching them to obey everything I have commanded you. And remember, I am with you always, to the end of the age." (Matt 28:18–20)

In this well-known passage alone, there are imperatives for the church that normally require the characteristics of an institution such as we have noted above. Notwithstanding the early church's sense of eschatological urgency, the great commission presumes some continuity through time and space "even to the end of the age." Well before Matthew's Gospel was written, the church was coming to understand its mission as continuing beyond the lifetime of some of its members (1 Thess 4:13–18). The call to make disciples across the diversity and spread of the Roman Empire (the nations) would clearly take not just organization, but time. In making disciples, the followers of Jesus are to hand on tradition (*paradosis*: "everything that I have commanded you"). They are to shape the lives of others ("make disciples . . . and teaching them") and in doing this, they are to use rituals of identity and belonging ("baptizing them in the name of the Father and of the Son and of the Holy Spirit"). It would, of course, be tenuous in the extreme to read into Matthew's account of the great commission some form of instruction from Jesus for the creation of a new institution.[8] If anything, as we shall see, Jesus saw himself as critiquing and fulfilling the existing institutions of the people of God. Nevertheless, it remains significant that those things that are outlined in Matthew as at the heart of the church's mission, so fully align with the sort of societal functions we have outlined above as being associated with the development of institutions.

In the incarnation, as Anglican theologian Dan Hardy puts it, Jesus enters not just a human life, but human sociality. As a (*the*) human being "fully in relationship with others," Jesus transforms "from within" human social life including those social structures that we call institutions.[9]

> From this point of view, the Church—in heaven and on earth—is the unfolding of what was accomplished in him for the full scope of human existence.

So far it has become evident that, not only are some of the key elements of the church's mission focused in activities and areas that often emerge in institutional expression within society, but that the fact of Christ becoming fully human (to use a modern rendering of words from the Nicene Creed) calls forth an expression of the transformation of the human social world within and through the church. In this sense, the institutional is not just a necessity for ministry in the world, but a sphere of its expression; salvation is not just for the individual, but for the "us-ness" of humanity in all its relationships, including those with the created order. Part of the church's mission is to model that call and wholeness in sociality.

Sadly, there are times when church communities are more toxic than other organizations in the world around them. This brings us back to Dan Hardy's word: "unfolding." It is a word that implies both incompleteness and gradual progress. In seeking to show forth Christ's way on earth, the church is "not there yet."[10] It looks to completion but expresses itself in

---

8. The term *ecclesia* occurs only twice in the Gospels, both times in Matthew (Matt 16:18 and 18:17). The phrase "the kingdom of God/heaven" occurs about a hundred times.

9. Hardy, *Finding the Church*, 33.

10. "Are we there yet?" I am picking up a popular slogan that was also the title of a 2005 American family comedy film directed by Brian Levant. A book by the same title was published in Australia in 2004, with Alison Lester being the author.

incompletion. Moreover, there is a temptation to idealize the unfolding of God's way through the church's community on earth as a steady progression, with consistent progress and each step being a step forward. Church history and even the reflections of the New Testament tell us that life in the "not-there-yet" of being the church is much messier than this, and that each hopeful step forward has the potential of not just the good, but "the good, the bad, and the ugly." There will be moments of walking in the sun and there will be moments of getting lost in the darkness, moments of breakthrough and moments of betrayal. Here we are brought back to the concerns of Brunner and Moltmann and recognize that the possibility for what they both called false developments are there with the church at every stage of its earthly journey and that even what might be seen as the most positive development will have what Hans Küng called a "dark shadow"—a latent possibility of distortion inseparably part of every historical expression short of the ultimate fulfillment of all things in the kingdom of God.[11]

> All ecclesiology must take as one of its bases, not merely the historicity of the church, but the fact that the church is historically affected by evil; and this fact must be accepted from the start without false apologetics and always taken into account. For this reason ecclesiology can never simply take the *status quo* of the church as its yardstick, still less seek to justify it. On the contrary, taking once again the original message, the Gospel, as its starting point, it will do all that it can to make critical evaluations as a foundation for the reforms and renewal which the church will always need.

Avery Dulles, in his influential volume *Models of the Church*, points out that the way the New Testament most commonly describes the church is in "revealing images."[12] The church is a building raised up by Christ, the house of God, the temple and tabernacle of God, God's people, God's flock, God's field and vine, a city, the bride of Christ, and the body of Christ. The power of images is that while they provide information they are also evocative. They convey but do not contain. They provide a picture, but also evoke the imagination of something more. Just as the church in its pilgrim journey is incomplete, so any one particular image, or model, of the church is incomplete and needs to be placed among others so that they "interpenetrate and mutually qualify one another."[13] Sometimes the truth of the

---

11. Küng, *Church*, 28.
12. Dulles, *Models of the Church*, 19–23.
13. Dulles, *Models of the Church*, 20–32.

church's being is only found when images are held together in "logically incoherent ways," that is, the truth is found in holding the differing images in tension without seeking to coalesce or collapse the differences.

The institutional model of the church

Beyond the exploration of biblical images of the church, Dulles is more well-known for his development of analogies from human experience into what he calls models, with each of the models calling attention to "certain aspects of the church that are less clearly brought out by other models."

> In selecting the term "models," rather than "aspects" or "dimensions," I wish to indicate my conviction that the church, like other theological realities, is a mystery. Mysteries are realities of which we cannot speak directly. If we wish to talk about them at all we must draw on analogies afforded by our experience of the world. These analogies provide models. By attending to the analogies and utilising them as models, we can indirectly grow in our understanding of the church.[14]

Without proposing his list as definitive, Dulles proposed five models of how the church is present in the world: as institution, mystical communion, sacrament, herald, and servant. In a revised edition he added a sixth model, that of the church as a community of disciples. The various models, suggests Dulles, are not to be integrated into a "synthetic vision" of the church, but because the church is a complex reality, they must be held together: "By a kind of mental juggling act, we have to keep several models in the air at once."[15] Every model has strengths and weaknesses, so each must be placed firmly into the context of the others, to "criticise each of the models in light of all the others" and refrain from "so affirming any one of the models as to deny, even implicitly, what the others affirm."[16] Even then, as Stephen Pickard points out, there is still the risk that the language of models can lean towards a "steady-state" approach to the being of the church, with insufficient recognition of the dynamic, movement, and energy of the church on its eschatological journey.[17]

---

14. Dulles, *Models of the Church*, 9–10.
15. Dulles, *Models of the Church*, 10.
16. Dulles, *Models of the Church*, 196.
17. Pickard, *Seeking the Church*, 44–49. "We are in a period of history when pluralism and diversity abound which means that the question of models of the Church will remain

Institutional or institutionalized?

In his initial list of five models, Dulles placed the institutional first, not because it was most important, but because "in the popular mind the Catholic Church is identified with what I describe as the institutional model of being church."[18] In later writing he recognized that putting the institutional first may have created the wrong impression, because the institutional was really a secondary aspect of being the church. Nevertheless, he maintained that its inclusion among his five models was necessary to a valid ecclesiology because the church was called into visible and historical form, with an organization and structure analogous to the organization of other human societies.[19]

The strength of the institutional model is that it takes seriously the historical reality of the church in the world within the reality of the world as it is. Even if it must claim to be more, the church is what theologians have called the "church visible"; the church as a people of faith belong together over time, attending to the necessities, both large and small, of people living together and relating to the structures of the world around them. It gives "skin and flesh" structure to faith in the present and a sense of visible continuity with the past.

This model also has some significant shortcomings. It encourages some virtues, such as loyalty and obedience, but it gives little space to the

---

a contested and essentially unfinished business. Of course, this may be precisely how it ought to be from a theological point of view" (44). Dulles actually says something similar. He concludes *Models of the Church* by suggesting "one final caution might be in order. Theologians often tend to assume the essence of the Church somehow exists, like a dark continent, ready-made and awaiting to be mapped. The Church, as a sociological entity, may be more correctly viewed as a 'social construct'. In terms of sociological theory, one may say that the form of the Church is constantly modified by the way in which members of the Church externalise their own experience and in so doing transform the Church to which they belong. Within the myriad possibilities left open by Scripture and tradition, the Church in every generation has to exercise options." Dulles, *Models of the Church*, 198–99.

To use a simple metaphor, the risk of thinking in terms of multiple models is to regard them as a jigsaw puzzle, which when put together provide a complete picture, when in fact for the church on its pilgrim journey, the pieces are constantly changing shape and number. The jigsaw is never complete, at least this side of the eschaton!

18. Dulles, *Models of the Church*, 10.

19. In an appendix to his 2002 revised edition of *Models of the Church*, Dulles seems to offer slight corrective over the earlier edition, making the point that although institutional expression was essential for the church, it was secondary, in that its role was to "preserve and promote communion" (224).

creative and prophetic. It tends towards the juristic and is conducive to the overdevelopment of hierarchy and clericalism, reducing the laity to a role of passive support, as the critique of Brunner and Moltmann so powerfully made clear. It can be monopolistic, triumphalist, and therefore ecumenically sterile.

Like all characteristics of the church, the institutional can be exalted from the provisional "not-yet" and "in-between" into the realms of the ideal. This is perhaps most clearly reflected in the characterization of the church within Roman Catholic theology as a "perfect society"—a term that was carefully nuanced, but which nevertheless contributed to a sense of the church being beyond critique and accountability.[20] As this "informal infallibility" becomes the approved way for clerical leaders and administrators to act, so structure becomes the end rather than the means of church life and the possibilities for the misuse of position and power increase.

The corrective Dulles proposes is to ensure that the institutional model, with its gift of order and structure, must be taken into, and indeed serve, the communal and organic—the church as a mystical communion, the church as a sacramental and diaconal community—if that institutional order and structure is not to become rigid and tyrannical.[21]

Here Dulles makes a helpful distinction between the necessity of institutional expressions within the life of the church and the development of "institutionalism." If the church begins to treat its institutional expression as primary and indispensable, then it strays into institutionalism. Pickard makes a similar, if slightly different, distinction when he talks about the risk of a certain model so dominating discourse and practice as to become a controlling paradigm.

When institutionalism becomes the church's primary self-understanding, then the shortcomings and distortions of institutional expression come to the fore. The gift of order becomes coercive. Leadership is possessed by a positional elite. Community yields to jurisdiction. Cooperation gives way to compliance. Structure becomes a rigid end in itself, subjugating all other functions, so that the teaching role of the church, for example, is limited to a defense of the institutional status quo and an often narrowly defined orthodoxy becomes a criterion for institutional membership and

20. The term was meant to signify that the church had all it needed for its own mission, not that the church was perfect in every way. Nevertheless, the great assurance of Jesus to the church is not that it would have in itself all that it needed, but that in its need "I will be with you to the end of the age."

21. Dulles, *Models of the Church*, 32, 196–98.

approval.[22] Identifying institutionalism as a distortion of the necessarily institutional allows us to revisit the warnings of Brunner and Moltmann of false development, where too much emphasis on the institutional leads to an inauthentic ecclesiology in which a great majority within the *ecclesia* are deprived of the responsibility of their holy calling. The truth of the being of the church is better apprehended when the tensions between these different aspects of its life are carefully maintained. This is a theme we will explore further.

Institution, institutionalism, power, and abuse

All human society involves the distribution of power and this in turn involves differentials in power.[23] Leaders emerge and positional power is established. Specialists emerge with knowledge that gives them leverage. At its most wholesome, power can be seen as an extension of consensus, the ability to put in place what politicians call "the will of the people."[24] It is rare, however, for any sizeable human entity to achieve complete unanimity, so the exercise of power in real life generally supports the position of some, at best a majority, while others may see their aspirations less adequately met. Even in the institution of the law, before which all are meant to be equal, there are those who have positional influence, or specialist knowledge, that might be seen to advantage them, though within a healthy society or institutions there are usually checks and balances to ensure that such advantages of position or knowledge are not used to the disadvantage of others. In human institutions, there are inevitably some differentials or inequalities of power, and while in most institutions those inequalities are moderated by various structures and conventions, wherever there are inequalities of power abuse can occur.[25]

Whatever might be said of institutions more generally can be said of institutional expressions within the church. Even where there is a prevailing

---

22. Dulles, *Models of the Church*, 44–46.
23. Sykes, *Power and Christian Theology*, 12–13.
24. Giddens, "'Power' in the Recent Writings of Talcott Parsons," 268.
25. Lawrence, "Power, Institutions and Organizations," 170. Lawrence makes the point that because part of the nature of institutions is that they perpetuate social practices, departures from which are subject to socially constructed controls. "Thus power, in the form of repetitively activated controls, is what differentiates institutions from other social constructions."

narrative of equality and mutual human service, the distribution of power within institutional expressions of the church will have at best a softened version of what goes on in the wider world. What the Australian royal commission made clear, however, was that the churches often had less by way of conventions and accountability structures to curb abuses of power than many institutions in the world around them. Furthermore, as we shall see, in the churches there is the particular risk that inequalities and abuses of power can go unrecognized and unaddressed precisely because of a prevailing narrative of equality and community ("that couldn't happen in our church!"). The dangers of idealizing the church will be explored further in subsequent chapters.

To link the possibility of abuse to institutional expressions is not to say that other models of church do not involve power, or the possibility of the abuse of power. The model of church as herald, as proposed by Dulles, emphasizes the kerygmatic, the church as proclaimer and teacher, but knowledge is power and the emphasis on proclamation can create its own sort of power elite. An emphasis on the church as a holy community, on the other hand, can produce a withdrawal into spiritual rigor where power can be manifested as the power to exclude those who are seen as compromised or lacking the necessary fervor.

On its own account, the church might regard itself as more than just another institution, but as Stephen Sykes suggests, "it can scarcely be denied that it has internal problems with the distribution and exercise of power at least analogous to those of other organizations. And it does not seem to cope with these better by denying that they exist, or refusing to see where they come from."[26]

To talk about problems associated with the distribution and exercise of power, however, is not to suggest that power is necessarily negative, or even always coercive. Power is, as Giddens put it, no more or less than the capacity to achieve outcomes.[27] Most often the use of power "represents a facility for the achievement of objectives that both sides in a power relation desire."[28] Critiquing earlier models of power in society, Talcott Parsons ar-

---

26. Sykes, *Power and Christian Theology*, 13.
27. Giddens, *Constitution of Society*, 257.
28. Giddens, "'Power' in the Recent Writings of Talcott Parsons," 263. Parsons argued that the creation of a power system did not necessarily entail the coercive subordination of the wishes or interests of one party to those of another. Rather, he argued, coercive power, or power with negative sanctions, was just one "channel" through which power worked in human institutions. Other "channels" he referred to were the offering of

gued that power in an organization could be more than a "zero-sum game," by which he was challenging the assumption that in the exercise of power, when one party wins, the other must lose. Social systems, he argued, actually generate power so that a "non-zero game" was possible; that is, when institutions function well, all parties stand to gain.[29]

Parsons's reminder that the exercise of power need not be negatively at the expense of others was an important corrective in its day; however, its modernist assumption of coherence and almost inevitable progress has received its own share of criticism as well. Modern social systems are extraordinarily complex, often inclusive of great diversity, and within them power is almost always a contested dynamic. Beyond the smaller social units such as the family and clan, the possibility of power being exercised to consistently produce "win-win" outcomes would seem remote. Healthy democracies function on the presumption that the institutions of democracy will produce at best the most "wins" for the most people, but as any politician will testify, there will always be some who feel disgruntled or alienated.

Institutions work through habitualized patterns of interaction that are not always receptive to the differently nuanced, the different, or exceptional. For all their necessity, and even at their best, the benefits that flow from them will have mixed in some of the negatives—unnecessarily coercive control, punishment of dissent, and even abuse.

There are two factors that magnify the risks of these negative aspects to institutional life and both of them have particular relevance to the church. Those factors are size and institutional longevity. Niklas Luhman points out that while in smaller groupings, power can be centralized around a person, and exercised in direct relationships, larger entities such as national and international religious institutions are forced to establish more complex systems, a legitimized power apparatus.[30] While such a system might offer more checks and balances than might be expected in a smaller institution, where power might be centered directly around an individual, there are disadvantages as well. There is the risk of what Max Weber called "formalistic impersonality," through which the workings of power can become remote and inaccessible, with decision-making almost always flowing in

---

positive inducements, the "intention channel" of offering good reasons for compliance, and the negative side of the "intention channel," the appeal to conscience or other moral commitments.

29. Giddens, "'Power' in the Recent Writings of Talcott Parsons," 258.

30. Luhmann, *Trust and Power*, 123. See also Weber, *Economy and Society*, 33–38, 212–15.

a top-to-bottom direction.[31] The legitimizing of power that is necessary for its effective working in any organization can morph into the legitimization of the organizational status quo and a self-protective resistance to accountability.

This tendency to distortion can grow as institutions age. Weber identified tradition as one of the elements that provide legitimation to institutions.[32] As an institutional story evolves over time into a venerable tradition, so the practices and structures supported by that tradition tend to become more rigid and fixed, less amenable to question and change.[33] There is probably no clearer example of an organization being legitimized though tradition than the church, with its emphasis on the authority of Scripture as well as its inheritance from its early institutional leaders and decision-making, all that being well-expressed in the well-worn Anglican formula of Scripture, tradition, and reason. In the case of the church, inherent institutional tendencies towards rigidity, a lack of accountability, and power distortions can be seen to have the ultimate legitimation: a link with the divine. The result can be the development of an institutional culture in which the possibility of abuse is heightened, and the resort to cover-up more likely.

"Getting over" the institutional church?

When my friend, after decades of service, said in a moment of frustration that he was "over the institutional church," I suspect he was reacting to the contestation and distortions of power, the organizational preoccupation and the obstructionist resorting to process that can be part of every institution, though in the church such things are often expressed under the cover of doctrinal disagreements.

In the end, however, there can be no "getting over" the institutional church, except to abandon the church altogether. While it is always called to be more, and is reminded of that through a multiplicity of biblical images, the only church is the church on earth and its enduring social forms will tend to be different only in degree from those of the world around it. When the church fails to recognize this, it moves to a place of peril. At the same time, in recognizing that the church cannot escape some form of

---

31. Weber, *Economy and Society*, 225–26.
32. Weber, *Economy and Society*, 36.
33. McCann, *Church and Organization*, 29–30.

institutional expression and that even the best institutions are capable of self-deception and distortion, there is the risk of a sort of "institutional resignation." There could be the temptation to take the attitude of "it is what it is" and to give up on questioning the church in its institutional expressions, or an end to seeking to improve them.

It is of the nature of every institution to resist any challenge to its prevailing narrative. The personal cost to whistle-blowers and even those in senior leadership within the church who called attention to issues of sexual abuse and cover-up has been well-documented, including in the Australian royal commission report.[34] To face the truth of what is itself often takes great courage, not just in confronting the actual misuse or abuse of power, but in identifying the institutional defaults that predispose the possibility of such abuse and of covering it up. Gerald Arbuckle describes it as a struggle between reality and rhetoric, or to put it more sympathetically, it means for many faithful people a difficult and sometimes costly laying down of idealizations of the church, often faithfully held, in order to come to the place of honesty from which healing might begin.[35]

> "Blessed are you who weep now, for you will laugh" (Luke 6:21). Yes, we need to weep now, acknowledging countless cultures of abuse over generations. Only then can we collectively begin to journey forward with the faith-based laughter of converting hearts.

From the place of honesty, the church can hear its vocational call once more. It is of the nature of the church that it must live, not only in the honesty of what now is, but in openness to the continuing challenge of what will be in the fullness of the kingdom of God. So just as denial and the resort to idealism is untrue to the nature of the church, so is uncritical acceptance of what is. The constant challenge, as Joseph McCann suggests, is to find the "good fit," by which he means those expressions that, within the constraints of human reality, best represent the values of the gospel.[36]

---

34. Commonwealth of Australia, Royal Commission Final Report, 32. The Final Report included multiple de-identified narratives describing the difficulties and trauma faced by those who were whistle-blowers within the church. In a section specific to the Anglican Church (volume 16) the royal commission notes that even senior church leaders attempting to address issues of abuse were subject to undermining and backlash.

35. Arbuckle, *Abuse and Cover-Up*, xvi–xix.

36. McCann, *Church and Organization*, 135. Avery Dulles suggested a set of criteria for evaluating the various models of the church; (1) basis in Scripture, (2) basis in Christian tradition, (3) capacity to give church members a sense of their corporate identity and mission, (4) tendency to foster the virtues and values generally admired by Christians,

For the church this can never be a settled thing, as the explorations of subsequent chapters will make clear.

---

(5) correspondence with religious experience today, (6) theological fruitfulness. The diversity of these criteria reinforces the fact that what is implied is a constant process of re-evaluation and reform. Dulles, *Models of the Church*, 191–92.

Chapter 3

DOMINION, DISTORTION, AND DOMINATION

CHURCH INSTITUTIONS DO NOT descend from heaven intact and perfect. One way or another, the institutional forms found within the people of God are largely adopted and adapted from their social context. Recognizing this does not set aside the possibility of a providential element in their development, or a sense of holiness in their expression, but it is to say that institutional expressions within the people of God carry many of the same advantages, risks, and possibilities for the distortion of power that are part of every human institution. This chapter will briefly explore further some of those tensions and ambiguities of power through the story of the people of God.

A detailed study of power through the biblical literature is well beyond the scope of this present exercise, so I will adopt the methodology of tracing the thread lightly through the text, pausing to examine significant patterns as they emerge. Faithfulness is found, it will be suggested, neither in the denial of power, nor in divinizing it, but in the grey space of tension and paradox, where the exercise of power and a self-conscious critique of that exercise of power are constant companions. Throughout the story of the people of God, when power is given divine endorsement and the prophetic critique of its use is suppressed, then the possibilities of distortion and abuse always loom large.

The Genesis analysis: dominion, domination, and division

Authority and power are among the elemental themes developed in the primeval history of Genesis 1–11. Often interpreted etiologically, or even descriptively, this section of the Bible is probably best seen as existential and interpretive. Rather than trying to address theoretical or abstract questions about origins, it seeks primarily to make a theological and pastoral response to a real historical problem, "to find a ground for faith in this God when the experience of sixth-century Babylon seems to deny the rule of this God."[1] More than an account of how things came to be, it is "an explanation of the way things are, with all its potential for good and ill."[2]

The context is a crisis of faith and cultural identity. Israel's brief national epoch had been dominated by great powers, and eventually brought to an end by them. Successive superpowers, Assyria and Babylon, sought to displace and assimilate peoples and annihilate national and cultural identities (2 Kgs 17:24–25). This experience of subjection and exile colors the Genesis primeval history with an ideological and oppositional edge. It is a narrative in "critical dialogue with the powers and ideologies of the region, and in life-or-death conflict with them."

> In this context, the oneness of Yahweh is more than an assertion of the rights of this god over against that god, more even than the means whereby a vulnerable people preserved its identity, but part of an alternative view of power and order in the world.[3]

Engaging with the cosmologies represented in the creation myths of the surrounding world, the biblical creation stories focus on Elohim/Yahweh as the sole, sovereign, and unqualified actor.

> The world came into being because God created, God said, God saw, God made a distinction, God called, God made, God put, God blessed, God finished, God made sacred, God stopped.[4]

The stately affirmation of Elohim/Yahweh's sole and sovereign act in creation is much more than an abstract contemplation on the nature of

---

1. Brueggemann, *Genesis*, 25–26. Most scholars now recognize that the primeval history, including the creation stories of Genesis, reached something close to final form during the Babylonian exile, and was interacting with the myths of imperial Babylon.
2. McConville, *God and Earthly Power*, 36.
3. McConville, *God and Earthly Power*, 20.
4. Goldingay, *Genesis*, 49.

supreme deity. It challenges the prevailing creation myths that underwrite and sacralize a human power system though a cosmology of hierarchy and conflict, with a high god and lesser deities identified with natural phenomena such as the sun and moon and the political rulers as semi-divine figures. The Genesis stories of creation redraw this cosmological map, with a clear distinction between the unqualified power of the divine and that of the natural order.[5] God is God. The lesser divinities of the Babylonian world, the heavenly systems, the sun, moon, and sky are parts of the natural order, not of a divine hierarchy that supports the oppressive reign of Babylon. The natural world is not animated and therefore is not a source of fear. On the contrary, it is the realm of human stewardship and work. The image of the divine is found, not in the person of the king or the king's statues, but in humanity's "us-ness," the sociality represented in Genesis with the male and the female together.[6] Coming from a people oppressed, the creation narrative in Genesis presents an alternative and subversive cosmology of order and power to that of Babylon, where human structures and even the forces of nature are divinized in a subjugating hierarchy of power.

In the alternative cosmology of Genesis, creation is crafted in orderly succession, culminating in the shaping like pottery of a human person; the earthling *adam* is crafted from the *adamah* earth to look after and work the *adamah*. It is humanity in sociality that is accorded the title of being an "image" of the divine and not one human as distinct from or over another (Gen 1:26). Thus humanity has dominion on the earth as the divine viceregent. The emphasis of meaning for the word "to have dominion," or "rule" (*radah*) is much debated among the scholars, particularly in regard to the extent to which it implies rule by force.[7] A consensus seems to be that while

---

5. McConville, *God and Earthly Power*, 24. There is no distinction here between a god of heaven and a god of earth (as in Babylon, between Ea and Anu, both in turn subject to En-Lil); or of the story of Marduk the chief god of the city of Babylon, who triumphs over the chaos of Tiamet to become Lord (*Bel, Baal*)of the lesser gods. In Babylon, primeval conflict between the gods led to the sustaining of order in the world through the victory of Marduk who reigned from Babylon. In this way creation ideology served to underwrite a political system.

6. McConville, *God and Earthly Power*, 26. The creation of humanity as "the image of God" (Gen 1:26–27) makes two distinct but related polemical points: the "image" (*tselem*) of God is to be found, not in manufactured idols, but in humanity, since Hebrew *tselem* is a standard word for such idols; moreover, it is humanity as a whole and not kings that enjoys royal status. Rather than being under domination by semidivine rulers, humans in community are given domination under God.

7. The different understandings of *radah* are illustrated in an exchange between two

there may be implicit force in the idea of dominion, it is above all God's dominion exercised by humanity in the role of vice-regents, and thus the nature of the rule must align with the purposes of God who regards all creation as good, and so the dominion that the humans are given is directed towards that good.[8] In contrast to the domination systems of ancient Babylon, in which human community is subjected to divinized power, Genesis offers an alternative worldview, where humans in equal community exercise a dependent dominion under God.

For the exiles in Babylon, the experience of dominion has been far from that of rule for the good. They have seen their nation invaded and ravaged. They have been deported as the result of a strategy of imperial assimilation and they live under a regime that legitimates its power through a pervasive cosmology. Their forming story needs to take account of this, and even more, respond to it, so Genesis 1–11 takes us on an anticipatory journey from the garden of beginnings to the ziggurats of Babylon. Again, we approach this story more as an interpretive description of life as it is, than as a theoretical inquiry into origins, or as a prescription of what shall be.

The earthlings are to "subdue" *(kabash*: keep within limits) the garden and its inhabitants, but one of the humans allows a creature to exceed its limits and exercise sway over her, breaching the order of their God-given dominion. The woman in turn breaches the God-set limitations of human dominion in the garden and the other human allows himself to be co-opted. They find themselves estranged from the garden of their origins, alienated from creation and from each other.

> To the woman God said,
> "I will greatly increase your pain in child-bearing;

Australian scholars, Norman Habel and Michael Stead. Habel argues that the human mandate to rule "involves the forceful exercise of power," whereas Stead's position is that in the absence of other qualifying words suggesting harshness or undue force, the word *radah* does not carry the connotation of harsh rule. In the creation stories *radah* is qualified by three other words: *kabash* "to subdue, or to trample down" (1:28), *adab* "to work or till" (2:15) and *shamar* "to keep or preserve" (2:15). Both *adab* and *shamar*, as they are used elsewhere carry a sense of respectful care. It does seem difficult to entirely avoid the notion of force, yet the emphasis seems to be on humanity ruling as God rules, wisely and benevolently. Habel, "Introducing Ecological Hermeneutics." Stead, "To 'Rule Over' and 'Subdue' the Creation." See also Brueggemann, *Genesis*, 25–32.

8. Brueggemann, *Genesis*, 32: "The 'dominion' here mandated is with reference to the animals. The dominance is that of a shepherd who cares for, tends, and feeds the animals. Or, if transferred to the political arena, the image is that of a shepherd-king (Ezek 34). Thus the task of 'dominion' does not have to do with exploitation and abuse."

> In pain you shall bring forth children.
> Yet your desire shall be for your husband
> And he shall rule over you." (Gen 3:16)

As the vice-regents of God the great King, the earthlings were to exercise shared dominion over creation for its good, but now dominion is no longer shared. It has become a dividing thing. The man exercises control over the woman. The Hebrew word here is *mashal*, a synonym of *radah*, but perhaps with a greater sense of direct control, such as the control that God uses to ensure that the heavenly bodies stay in place (Gen 1:18).[9] Despite the male taking what was to be shared between them and exercising it in a controlling way, the woman's desire is for him still. The text here is interesting, and taking a cue from Gen 4:7, a more provocative paraphrase might be offered, based on a similar translation of the same word for desire (*teshukah*) as in the Genesis 4 passage.

> Your desire will be to control your husband,
> but he shall exercise control over you.

Even setting aside this less conventional translation, the Genesis analysis of power is clear; outside the garden of God, power and dominion tend toward domination and division. The sharing of human power founded in paradise is replaced by differentiation, domination, and competitive struggle. As the narrative progresses the description of distortion embraces the characteristic expressions of the whole of human society; the family (Gen 4:1–16), kinship (Gen 4:17–25), labor (Gen 4:2–7), nations (Gen 10), and the city (Gen 11:1–9).

The primeval history journeys from the garden of God to the great city of Babylon. Maintaining our approach that sees this part of Genesis more about interpreting how things are than detailing origins, the culmination of this section of Genesis in Babylon is significant. This is where the exiles are. This is the reality of their world and the Genesis narrative engages with it. In the garden of the ideal there is harmonious order, equality and fruitfulness at every level, but in the world that humans now inhabit, order is distorted, dominion is expressed in domination and hierarchy, and fruitfulness is hard won and often competitively so.

This is the world recognized as it is, and retreat from that human reality back into the garden of the ideal is forbidden with a fiery sword. Yet

---

9. Foh, "What Is the Woman's Desire," 381–83. The early fathers tended to translate the word as "turn"; the woman will turn to the man in all things, thus allowing dominion.

at the same time, there is a critique of the world as it is, with its abusive excesses. As a narrative that culminates in the place of oppression (Babylon), the primeval history recognizes that human sociality tends always to be marked by distortions of the garden ideal, but it refuses to deify those distortions. The hierarchical cosmology of Babylon is rejected, as is the deification of human power systems. The primeval history leaves us with no retreat to the idealized forbidden, and the deification of things as they are rejected. Human life is to be lived in the in-between, in the tension between un-divinized reality and the critique of that reality through an ideal that must be maintained but cannot be a place of retreat.

The ideal and the actual

The tension between the "is" and "ought" of power continues to be examined through what has been called the Deuteronomistic history.[10] Within this collection, the book of Deuteronomy has the function, at least in part, of projecting the ideal. As Mark Brett puts it, Deuteronomy presents a utopian model for a nation that has little parallel in the historical. It imagines a nation where class divisions are minimized, where there is special care for the vulnerable, the alien, the widow and orphan, and the king is a constitutional monarch, living in covenant relationship with both the people and God.[11]

> The people are configured not so much as subjects of a king as citizens of a "constitutional theocracy," knit together by bonds of kinship. Not only are the social divisions of everyday experience relativized in this social theory, but a separation of powers is envisaged in ways that cohere astonishingly well with modern conceptions of nationalism.

What follows is a contrast to this ideal. The tension between the actual and ideal, between the "is" and the "ought" is played out through the Deuteronomistic history in the relationship between successive kings and the prophets of God. In a somewhat tongue-in-cheek reflection on the choice

---

10. Nineteenth-century scholars noted thematic and literary connections between the books of Deuteronomy, Joshua, Judges, 1 and 2 Samuel, and 1 and 2 Kings, suggesting that this part of the Bible was brought to a completion sometime after the Babylonian conquest of Jerusalem in 587–586 BCE, and reflecting a theological understanding of what brought about the fall of Israel and Judah.

11. Brett, *Locations of God*, 38, 50–53.

of Saul as the first king of Israel (1 Sam 8:1–22), McCann captures the tension. The Israelites are facing a double crisis. They are under constant pressure from the military superiority of the Philistines and there is no clear succession of leaders in Samuel's sons, who "did not follow in his ways." They want to transition to a more able and more stable form of government, a monarchy "like the other nations."[12]

Samuel, the priest, prophet, and judge, is called in as a "management consultant" and takes the demand of the people to God. God accedes to the request for a king, while characterizing it as a rejection of his own kingship. Samuel is told to tell the people what the earthly institution of monarchy will be like. He pulls no punches. The rule of the king will be exercised in domination and compulsion.

> He will take your sons and appoint them to his chariots . . . he will take your daughters to be perfumers and cooks and bakers . . . he will take the best of your fields . . . and in that day you will cry out because of your king. (1 Sam 8:10–18).

In transitioning from the charismatic and organizational into the institutional rule of monarchy there are advantages and benefits for Israel that, almost three millennia later, sociologists would name in different language as the benefits of human institutionality: cohesion and identity (Durkheim), a focusing of energy (Weber), a holding together despite conflict and complexity (Parsons). But in the necessary, there is a loss of the ideal: "they have rejected me from being king over them." The transition is necessary. God gives it assent but not blessing and therefore it is a transition into an ambiguous reality. The exercise of earthly power is given divine permission but not divine endorsement. As a construct of human necessity, it will deliver its benefits, but always with them the risk of exploitation. Faithfulness is to be found in living out the tension between the aspiration of fulfillment and the reality of unfulfillment, between wheat and weeds, between the "beauty of holiness" and the too often unholy.

Following on from the dynamic between Saul and Samuel, David finds himself confronted by the prophet Nathan. When David plans to build a temple, Nathan delivers God's response, refusing the king's offer to build him a house and in that move co-opting God to bolster his reign (2 Sam 7:4–7).[13] David's adultery with Bathsheba elicits from the prophet

---

12. McCann, *Church and Organization*, 161.

13. God asserts his rule over the ruler. David will not build God a house. God will build David's house. Interestingly Nathan continues to call David *nagid* (prince) not

Nathan a word of divine judgment on David, matching the promise of dynastic succession "forever" with another "forever"—that of a sword always within his own house (2 Sam 12:10).[14] In David accepting the divine judgment, the often tense balance of prophet and king is maintained. The tension between the "is" of rule in Israel and the prophetic "ought" continues unabated through Israel's national epic and the potential of kingship to become tyrannical "like the nations" is highlighted by one prophet after another. Only Hezekiah and Josiah are portrayed as approaching the ideal, and then with qualifications. The transience and provisionality of Israel and Judah's structures of power are emphatically emphasized as they pass away and no political structures remaining except those imposed from outside.[15] With postexilic Israel ruled by governors and vassal kings, the ideal of king and kingdom is projected forward into eschatological expectation.[16]

The Old Testament texts we have examined provide a nuanced theological assessment of the disposition of power in human community, with pragmatic reality checked by higher ideal. Outside of paradise, human power will be exercised inevitably in differentiation and degrees of inequality. This is the human reality and even Israel is not exempt. It, too, will have rule like the nations. In Israel, however, that rule is held to prophetic account and it cannot be deified; only God is king and God holds earthly rule accountable. Nor can there be a retreat from the realities of earthly power into idealism; the way back to paradise is blocked by an angel and the function of the ideal is to provide critique, not escape. The nations might deify power and exercise it oppressively, but although the people of God live in this world of distorted power, they have a vocation to chart a different path. Their call is to live in the tension between the pragmatic necessity of having rule like the nations, with the inevitable distortions and differentiations that are part of earthly power, while at the same time holding a vision of rule under God that checks, critiques, and constrains the exercise of power as it tends towards abuse and oppression.

---

melek (king), emphasizing that God is *melek* and David rules as God's *nagid*.

14. McConville, *God and Earthly Power*, 142.
15. McConville, *God and Earthly Power*, 161.
16. Anderson, *Living World of the Old Testament*, 510, 626.

Polarities of power—the New Testament tension

In a book called *Power and Christian Theology*, Stephen Sykes suggested that the Christian tradition is marked by polarity and tension in its treatment of power, with different tendencies "pulling in opposite directions."[17] Following that thread of tension through the New Testament text, we will focus once more on some key passages and themes.

In the Gospels Jesus is presented as no stranger to power. He was born of the Virgin Mary who had been "overshadowed" by the power of the Most High (Luke 1:35). He commences his ministry filled with the power of the Spirit (Luke 4:14). He commands even the unclean spirits and they obey him, so that he is recognized as a prophet powerful in deed and word (Mark 1:27; Luke 24:19). He speaks of the Son of Man coming "with great power and glory" (Matt 24:31).

The ambiguity of power is also no stranger to him. In the wilderness experience that precedes his public ministry he rejects as diabolical the temptation to use his unique identity and power to serve his own purposes. Throughout his ministry he rejects repeated calls from critics and admirers alike that he perform deeds of power to establish his credentials.[18] In the shadow of death, and faced with the coercive power of Governor Pilate, he maintains his integrity in silence and points out that all human power is derivative (John 19:10–11). After avowing that his kingdom "is not of this world," he is crucified under a political title, "the King of the Jews" (John 18:36; 19:19).

"It is not so among you"

The Gospel passage most often represented as a rejection of earthy power by Jesus is Mark 10:35–46. Here Jesus points to the sort of rule exercised by the political rulers of the day and calls the disciples to a different way; whoever wants to be great must be a servant, and whoever wishes to be first must be slave of all. The context in Mark for Jesus addressing his disciples in this way is provided by a dispute between them in Capernaum about who among them was the greatest (9:34). On that occasion Jesus had responded to their wrangling about greatness with words about service and the example of a child. Apparently this was not enough to end the dispute, for it

---

17. Sykes, *Power and Christian Theology*, 28.
18. Feldmeier, *Power, Service, Humility*, 20.

surfaces again with John and James lobbying Jesus to "do for us whatever we ask of you" (10:35).

Perhaps remembering something of Jesus' previous response to the argument among the disciples who was the greatest, they mask their question. They want a blank check, a victor's payout "when you come in your glory." Instead of granting their deliberately vague request, Jesus asks what it is they actually want. Their ambitions are unmasked. They want the places of honor; one at the right and one of the left "in your glory" (10:37). The response of Jesus is twofold; James and John do not understand what they are asking for and in any case what they want is not his to grant. They do think they know what they are asking for; they equate glory with kingdom and kingdom with earthly, national rule.[19] They are not far off when they equate glory with kingdom, but as Mark consistently shows, the disciples are slow to grasp the radical inversion that is the true nature of that kingdom.[20] In any event, says Jesus, the places of honor are not his to grant but are for those for whom they are already prepared.

The rest of the disciples show themselves no less prone to naked ambition in their response to James and John. Their annoyance seems not to be at the inappropriateness of the ambition displayed by the two brothers, but at the possibility that somehow they might have been gazumped by them in lobbying for the places of honor.

The Markan story of the two brothers and their ambitious request is followed closely in Matthew, although the evangelist does "airbrush" the image of James and John by having the request come from their mother's lips. Luke does not refer to the request from the brothers, probably conflating the two stories in Mark and referring only to a dispute among the disciples as to who was the greatest (Luke 22:24–27). In each of the Synoptics the response of Jesus is similar.

> Jesus called them and said to them, "You know that among the Gentiles those whom they recognize as rulers lord it over them and their great ones are tyrants over them. But it is not so among

---

19. Painter, *Mark's Gospel*, 148–50.

20. Painter, *Mark's Gospel*, 148. Theodore Weeden suggests that Mark shows the disciples moving from "unperceptiveness" to "misconception" to "rejection" in regard to the nature of the ministry of Jesus. They run away from the moment of glory, which comes in the form of the suffering and cross, so that the final words of recognition are left to a Roman centurion, while the women followers watch on at a distance. Luke adds the irony that it is two thieves who are finally found at Jesus' right hand and left. Weeden, *Mark*, 23–51.

you; but whoever wishes to become great among you must be your servant, and whoever wishes to be first among you must be slave of all." (Mark 10:42–43)

This passage has often been used as a basis for the rejection of what Sykes calls "mundane power" among the people of God; "not power, but service." The two are put in opposition and during the twentieth century an ecclesiology of the "servant church" evolved around this binary approach. As a corrective, this movement made an undoubted contribution. However, a closer read would suggest that authenticity is to be found, not by constructing an extreme polarity between service and power, but in negotiating the more uncertain places in between.

Outside of the original garden, and short of the eschaton, human life is marked by human power in differentiation. Even in the Gospel exchanges between Jesus and his disciples about power and ambition, this has its recognition.

> Teacher, we want you to do for us whatever we ask of you. (Mark 10:42)

> Do you know what I have done to you? You call me teacher and Lord and you are right; that is what I am. (John 13:12)

Just as he addresses the will to distorted power among his disciples, Jesus himself accepts titles of power differentiation before going on to qualify them with radical values: "serve," "give," "ransom." Luke provides his own unique accompaniment to Jesus' rejection of distorted power. Where he records the rebuff by Jesus of the wrangling and aspirations to honor and power among his disciples, he follows up with an eschatological affirmation:

> You are those who have stood by me in my trials; and I [*now*] confer on you, just as my Father has [*previously*] conferred on me a kingdom [*kingly rule*], so that you may eat and drink at my table in my kingdom, and you will judge the twelve tribes of Israel. (Luke 22:28)

The tenses in this section are instructive. Having just chastised the disciples for their naked ambition, warning them of the sort of tyrannical rule that was the way of the "great ones" in the world around them, Jesus actually goes on to confer a rule upon them. In the context of the covenant language of the Last Supper, the language behind the word "confer" hints at will and covenant.²¹ The confronting irony of Luke's conjunctions of these pericopes is underlined by his use of the present tense for the word "confer." The disciples have been engaged in unseemly wrangling over position and honor and it is soon after this unflattering moment that they are formally told they will indeed rule and judge (lead) the regathered Israel. Despite the politics of preferment, Jesus confers an ordering of leadership among his people and surprisingly it is upon those whose inadequacies have just been prominently displayed.

Within the passage itself the reference by Jesus to "rulers" and "great ones" reflects the political language of the Graeco-Roman world. There is a hint of ambivalence in the phrase translated in the NRSV as "whom they recognize as their rulers"; it could equally be translated as "who are supposed to be their rulers," suggesting that their rule is other than it should be.²² More pointed is the phrase "lord it over" (*katakuriow*). The prefix (*kata*) gives it intensity and negativity. This is not just rule, it is rule exercised oppressively even against the best interest of the other, which is tyranny. The remedy to power exercised as tyrannical rule, says Jesus, is emulation of the one who came "not to be served but to serve" (*diakonein*).

The word *diakonia* here is often narrowly portrayed as the lowly service of table waiting, but as John Collins made clear in an exhaustive lexical study, the meaning of *diakonia* is much broader and can itself be inclusive of leadership roles, although usually on behalf of a higher ruler or divinity.²³ The oppositional polarity in Mark is not between service and power, but between abusive power and power used for the good of the other. Mark's frank description of the will to power among the disciples of Jesus allows no idealizing of those who lead in the Christian community, but nor does it encourage the denial of power under the language of service. For leaders among the people of God the one is exercised through the other. This is the understanding reflected by the author of 1 Peter, as he picks up the language of Mark in speaking about the role of presbyters within the church. They are to tend the flock of Christ in their charge "exercising the oversight, not under compulsion, but willingly . . . not for sordid gain, but eagerly. Do

---

21. The Greek word translated as "confer"(διατίθημι) can have the sense of "will" or "covenant" and the use earlier word of the word "covenant" (διαθηκη) would suggest a certain solemnity to Jesus' words here.

22. The word δοκοῦντες (δὸκεω-*dokein*) can have a slightly ironic sense here; they are "considered" to be rulers, although all rule belongs to God. For a useful discussion, see Cranfield, *Gospel According to Saint Mark*, 340.

23. Collins, *Diakonia*, 46–62.

not lord it over those in your charge [*katakuriow*—the same word that Jesus uses in Mark], but be examples to the flock of Christ" (1 Pet 5:1–2).

Finally, it is important to note that in Mark, the approach from James and John seeking places of honor comes immediately after a note that they were on the road, going up to Jerusalem.

> See we are going up to Jerusalem, and the Son of Man will be handed over to the chief priests and the scribes, and they will condemn him to death; then they will hand him over to the Gentiles; they will mock him and spit upon him. And flog him and kill him; and after three days he will rise again. (10:32–34)

As the Son of Man on the cross gives his life as "a ransom for many," not only is self-serving power exposed and denied, but a different power is expressed: the power of sacrifice. This is a theme powerfully developed by Paul.

Power and the powers

The letters of Paul are amongst the very early writings of the New Testament and come from a time when structures of belonging and leadership within the church were at an early stage of evolution. This has sometimes led to an idealization of the church of these times as charismatic and communal, with a mutuality of power lost in later times.[24] For all that the Pauline churches did have this more charismatic nature, however, there can be no denying the sort of individual power that Paul could wield, pronouncing judgement on a member guilty of immorality and requiring that he be "handed over to Satan for the destruction of the flesh" (1 Cor 5:5), and in the face of criticism claiming that he could, if necessary, confront the claims to power of those who oppose him, "not with words but a rod" (1 Cor 4:21). For Paul there is a legitimate use of power in the church to correct and protect, although characteristically this sort of power is a measure of last resort.

Likewise, Paul urges submission to the power of the governing authorities as "appointed by God" to bear the sword and maintain order. Believers are to pay taxes and duties as due and to offer honor and respect

---

24. Moltmann, *Church in the Power of the Spirit*, 305. Moltmann argues that the development of the monarchical episcopate was an error because it "quenched the Spirit," replacing the interdependence and mutuality of the charismatic church with a clerical monotheism.

to those who rule (Rom 13:1–7). Paul gives place for the exercise of power in the church and through the civil authorities. The apostle's acceptance of the exercise of power through the governing authorities and even within the church, however, is not without significant qualification. It is accompanied by a complex critique of the workings and structures of power and their capacity to enslave and take captive. Paul develops a minor lexicon to describe these realities. There are the "rulers," "authorities," "the cosmic powers of this present darkness," "spiritual forces of evil," against which the faithful are to stand strong and firm (Eph 6:10–17). There is "the Law" and also the "elemental spirits" through which believers can come into captivity (Gal 4:3; Col 2:8).

As Chris Forbes points out, it is easy to presume that this language in Paul means much the same as the references to demons and evil spirits in the Gospels and Acts, but during the second half of the twentieth century, and particularly following the manifestations of inhumanity and suffering in what was considered to be "civilized Europe"—on the western front during World War 1, or in Nazi Germany—there was a major reconsideration of the Pauline terminology.[25] Reflecting on his own experience in Europe during Hitler's ascendancy, Hendrikus Berkhof was massively influenced by the way that the powers of the time could take hold of the lives of millions of people: "No one could withhold himself, without utmost effort . . ." The influence of these powers was pervasive, inescapable; they were "in the air."[26] Berkhof argued that the Pauline "world powers" referred not to personal angels or demons, but to "the solid structures within which the pagan and Jewish societies of the day lived."[27] At their best they are the structures that hold life back from chaos. They might be the guardians and guides of human living, yet in overreaching they become tyrannical. The social necessity of human power structures opens up captivity to "the powers."

This approach was developed and popularized by Walter Wink, whose books included a trilogy, *Naming the Powers* (1984), *Unmasking the Powers* (1986), and *Engaging the Powers* (1992). Wink argued that a preoccupation within traditional biblical scholarship with the "personified aspects of power" did less than full justice to the biblical text, which in many instances was better understood as including the structural and social.

---

25. Forbes, "Paul's Principalities and Powers."
26. Berkhof, *Christ and the Powers*, 42–43.
27. Berkhof, *Christ and the Powers*, 28.

> What I propose is viewing the spiritual Powers not as separate heavenly or ethereal entities, but as the inner aspect of material or tangible manifestations of power.[28]

The Pauline language, then, of "principalities and powers," Wink suggests, should be seen as referring to "the inner or spiritual essence, or gestalt, of an institution, state or system." To say this, he argues, is not to suggest that "the powers" are mere personifications of institutional qualities. They are not mere hypostatizations or projections. The "powers" working through a human institution are much more than the combined power of those involved in that institution, since through their "greater duration and magnitude of power" institutions can take on a momentum of their own. "The powers we are speaking about are real. They work on us whether we acknowledge them or not."[29]

> A contractor pays off a building inspector so he can violate code and put up a shoddy and unsafe structure. A power plant exposes its employees to radioactive poisoning; the employee who attempts to document these safety infractions is forced off the road by another car and dies. All her documents are missing. Welcome to the world of the Powers.
> But the Powers aren't always that brutal. Some people enjoy their jobs. Some businesses make genuine contributions to society. Some products are life-enhancing, even life-saving. The Powers don't simply do evil. They also do good. Often they are both good and evil at the same time. They form a complex web that we can neither ignore or escape.[30]

Like the civil powers to which Paul urges submission, "the powers" come from God. They are created and are part of the fundamental ordering of the world (Col 1:15–17, 2:15–19).[31] They have a role for the whole of

---

28. Wink, *Naming the Powers*, 104.

29. Wink, *Naming the Powers*, 136. There are scholars who feel that Wink goes too far in seeming to remove altogether individual or personal spiritual beings from his understanding of the Pauline powers. For a more conservative approach, see O'Brien, "Principalities and Powers." This debate will undoubtedly continue, but does not affect the point being made, that the Pauline language points to the magnification and distortion of power through human organization and structures.

30. Wink, *Powers That Be*, 2.

31. This picks up the Greek of the phrase often translated "all things hold together in him," where the verb is συνέστηκεν (to put in place, to make part of a system). It also provides one possible and contextually reasonable translation of the much debated word, στοιχεῖα (Gal 4:3, 9 and Col 2:8, 20). Often translated as "elemental spirits," the basic idea

humanity such as the Law has for the Jewish people; they are guardians and pedagogues, although still just a "shadow of what is to come" (Gal 4:2–4; Col 2:17). Yet because they are so pervasive, touching the basic elements of human life, "the powers" can become enslaving, whether through a sense of astral determinism, religious observances, or the bonds of human tradition and thinking. The "powers" can assume the place of gods in human life. But on the cross, says Wink, the powers are "unmasked." They are shown for what they are. In the eschatological fulfilment, when Christ is all in all, they will take their place, reconciled and restored (Eph 1:10; Col 1:12–20).

> For I am convinced that neither death, nor life, nor angels, nor rulers, nor things present, nor things to come, nor powers, nor height, nor depth, nor anything else in all creation will be able to separate us from the love of God in Christ Jesus. (Rom 8:38–39)

Distorting powers inside the church

The contributions of Berkhof, Yoder, Wink, and others have opened up new perspectives on salvation as social and structural as well as personal. As a result of their work, the language of Paul was no longer dismissed as antiquated, but echoed with a new resonance into a world increasingly perplexed by the complexity of evil, and individuals whose lives felt more and more at the disposal of powers beyond their control.

Much of the interpretation of the biblical passages about "the powers" has been directed out, beyond the church to the world. For people like Berkhof, it provided a new way of seeing the gospel message in the context of social evil, such as was presented by Nazism. For Wink, it provided a theological base and methodology to address "the domination system" in the world at large: apartheid in South Africa, civil rights in the United States. This is entirely legitimate, of course. Yet the confronting reality is that many of the New Testament passages about principalities and powers and their human structures are directed in the first instance at what is happening *within* the church. At Galatia, the believers are at risk of abandoning the gospel gift of human freedom only to fall back into slavery to

---

is of being ordered "stitched together." It is sometimes understood as a reference to the basic elements of the universe, sometimes to basic teaching, and sometimes to spiritual powers. In each of these interpretations of *stoicheia* there remains the sense of an order or ordering that imposes itself on humanity and in the Pauline texts it is closely linked with the language of "powers."

human systems; the "elemental spirits" and the requirements of Jewish Law (Gal 1:6, 4:1–11). At Colossae, members of the church are at risk of being taken captive by human systems of thinking or rigorous religious regulations and observances, "festivals, new moons and sabbaths," according to the "elemental spirits of the universe" (Col 2:8–1, 20–23). Writing to the Ephesians, Paul concludes a long section in which he addresses issues like moral impurity, drunkenness, family relationships, and the treatment of slaves with the admonition that the church community should "put on the whole armor of God."

> For our struggle is not against enemies of blood and flesh, but against the rulers, against the authorities, against the cosmic powers of this present darkness, against the spiritual forces of evil in the heavenly places. (Eph 6:10–12)

This injunction by Paul should not be read in total disconnection to that which precedes it. The church's call to battle against the distorting powers has its first focus *within* the church. Even if the story of the people of God reveals a tendency to justify distortions within and critique those outside, from the New Testament perspective it is as the church first addresses the distorting powers within, so it addresses the world.[32]

A similar perspective may be found in the Revelation to John, where the churches of Asia are both encouraged and chastised; but no, it is not the churches that are addressed, rather it is their "angels"; the spiritual authority within each community that today might find partial description in the word "culture."

> And to the Angel of the church in Sardis write: "These are the words of him who has the seven spirits of god and the seven stars: I know your works; you have a name of being alive, but you are dead. Wake up and strengthen what remains!" (Rev 3:1–2)

In its high vocation, the church will be the instrument through which the wisdom of God is made known to the "rulers and authorities in the heavenly places" (Eph 3:10). Having this place in the divine plan, however, does not put the church outside the struggle, nor does it put the struggle outside the church. As we have seen from the Gospels through to the book

---

32. The Greek τοῦ λοιποῦ (for the rest) has the sense of summarizing what went before, as well as looking forward. The implication of this is to link the distortions in relationships within families, as well as the exploitation of slaves that the author addresses within the church, with the bigger picture of the church's struggle against the powers.

of Revelation, the disciples of Jesus are far from immune to the seductions and distortions of power, whether at the individual or communal level. To the extent that the church has an institutional reality, it is very much part of the power complex that Paul describes as "the powers." The church cannot simply project the distortion of power as something beyond itself. The witness to the wisdom of God cannot be in a church that somehow sees itself as apart from the distortions of power, but in a church engaged in self-reflective struggle against those distortions, firstly within, but also in the world around it.[33]

The powers, the cradle, and the cross

Jürgen Moltmann wrote a book of sermons called *The Power of the Powerless*. It includes a Christmas homily called "The Disarming Child."[34]

> The kingdom of peace comes through a child, and liberation is bestowed on the people who become as children: disarmingly defenceless, disarming through their defencelessness, and making others defenceless because they themselves are so disarming.
> After the prophet's mighty visions of the destruction of all power and the forceful annihilation of all coercion, we are suddenly face to face with this inconspicuous child.
> For what the prophet says about the eternal peace of God which satisfies our longings can only come to meet us, whether we are frightened slaves or aggressive masters, in the form of a child. A child is defenceless. A child is innocent. A child is the beginning of new life. His defencelessness makes our armament superfluous. We can put away our rifles and open our clenched fists . . .

In the incarnation God comes "disarmed," addressing the powers by self-disempowering; "he emptied himself, taking the form of a slave, being born in human likeness" (Phil 2:7). Yet "the powers that be" decreed the place of his birth (Luke 2:1) then sought to kill him as a baby to prevent him growing to become a political rival (Matt 2:1–18). When, as an adult, he assumed a public role, the scribes, representatives of the Law, used the institution of the Law to harass him. The priests, servants of the temple, conspired to bring him down. The Pharisees, personifying piety, persecuted him and cast him out of the synagogue. Finally, Pilate, institutional

---

33. Cobble, *Church and the Powers*, 5.
34. Moltmann, *Power of the Powerless*, 33–34.

representative of Roman justice and power, washes his hands of the truth and hands him over to death.[35]

The powers, "the rulers of this world" impose on Jesus during his earthly life, as they do on every human, but his response is neither one of aggression or complicity. He will not be part of the "pendulum swing of attack and revenge." He offers it no validity.

> [H]e does no violence, he utters no condemnation, he has no will to exclude or diminish. So John interprets the simpler themes of universal mercy and non-resistance. It is this which enables us to see emerging the image of the one who in any violent relationship can only be victim.[36]

He is the archetypal victim yet he will not be victimized. So when he stands before the representative of the greatest earthly power at the time, the Roman governor Pilate, he does so in shocking silence.

> "Where are you from?" But Jesus gave him no answer. Pilate therefore said to him, "Do you refuse to speak to me? Do you not know that I have the power to release you, and power to crucify you?" (John 18:8–11)

He offers no defense. He engages no "counter-violence" of a verbal or any other form.[37] "When he suffered, he did not threaten" (1 Pet 2:23). In face of the power that presumes to hold him, he does nothing more than name the distortion that can co-opt any power to "the powers."

> You would have no power over me unless it had been given you from above. (John 19:8–12)

It is a dethroning of sorts. Pilate sits on the judgment seat, but the impassive response of the one before him takes his power away and he can do little more than yield to the circumstances with a washing of hands. Jesus is taken away to the cross and all the "powers that be" have played their part: empire, politics, law, the military, religious scholarship and piety, the temple and priesthood. He is their victim, the sacrificial lamb, the scapegoat needed because human institutions are more ready to sacrifice an individual than for their ongoing existence to be put at risk (John 11:50). But

---

35. Berkhof, *Christ and the Powers*, 50.
36. Williams, *Resurrection*, 11.
37. Williams, *Resurrection*, 14.

his innocent nonresistance has taken their legitimacy away, as the writer to the Colossians put it:

> He disarmed the rulers and authorities and made a public example of them, triumphing over them in it. (Col 2:15)

There is support for an alternate reading here and it offers an even more provocative image:

> He divested himself (stripped off) of the rulers and authorities, showing them for what they are, and leading them in victory.[38]

In the Roman world it was common for the victorious to humiliate conquered forces by "stripping off" their armor. Here, we might see the writer proposing a radical and reverse proposition. Christ gains victory because he strips off his own armor! His innocent self-giving is the ultimate human divestment of power, and in that sacrifice, the powers and their legal legitimacy are nailed to the cross.

The new community: negotiating the powers

The cross of Christ, his self-sacrifice, is community creating. Yet that community too was "enmeshed with the network of powers" of its social situation. After Easter, the powers that imposed themselves on Jesus also impose themselves on his followers and the way of Jesus before the powers inspires their response.[39]

> The early communities, as they reproduced themselves in the ancient world in a variety of new contexts, saw the closest connection between Jesus' death and the new attitudes needed to sustain their community. They taught the absolute necessity of humility. There were to be no "rabbis" or "fathers" or "teachers." There was to be but one teacher, the Messiah, who conducted himself with

---

38. With the verb ἀπεκδυσαμενος there is a question as to whether the subject is "God" or "Christ." If Christ is the subject, then it may mean "stripping off from himself," as a person takes off clothes. This is the sense that the word is used at 3:9, where it is said that the believers have "stripped off the old self." An understanding based on the subject being Christ was favored in the early church.

In the Roman world it was common for the victorious to humiliate conquered forces by "stripping off" their armor. Here, we might see Paul proposing a radical and reverse proposition. Christ gains victory because he strips off his own armor! See Karris et al., *Colossians and Philemon*, 111.

39. Sykes, *Power and Christian Theology*, 130–31.

humility (Matt 23:8–12). Rivalry and personal vanity were to be given up. Christ's humility in accepting death by crucifixion was to inform their bearing towards one another (Phil 2:5–11).

Luke, in particular, teases out the parallels between the authorities that pursue and persecute Jesus and those that soon after Easter begin to persecute the church. In characteristic Lukan style, the author uses an element of repetition to emphasize the importance of his story for the early church, telling of the imprisonment and trial of the apostles (Acts 4:1–22, 5:24–42). The uneducated and ordinary stand before the assembled powers, the "rulers, elders and scribes" assemble, with Annas, Caiaphas, and "all who were of the high priestly family" (4:5) in the very city where "both Herod and Pontius Pilate, with the Gentiles and the people of Israel gathered together against your holy servant Jesus" (4:27). Luke's linking is explicit; the disciples stand before the powers "in this city" as Jesus did and in doing so they are vindicated.

> The intimidation and violence of the assembled powers do not succeed, "as they left the council, they rejoiced that they were considered worthy to suffer dishonor for the sake of the name" (5:41).[40]

In the Acts account of the conversion of Paul, a similar theme is developed. Paul, who has been persecuting the church on behalf of the religious authorities, is stopped in his zealous pursuit by a blinding light and an accusing voice (Acts 9:1–17).

> He responds—as might be expected—by addressing his accuser as "Lord" (9: 5), recognizing the hand of God in the event by which he is challenged and judged. And the reply identifies this "Lord" as "Jesus, whom you are persecuting." The Lord names himself not only as Jesus, but as Jesus embodied, in particular, in the present

---

40. Williams, *Resurrection*, 8–9. Williams notes how many of the elements of the trial of Jesus are present. Here it is as Jesus is present once more, but this time the victim is the judge. "The apostles stand in the name of Jesus before the court that condemned Jesus: to this court they must in turn pronounce the sentence of God, the sentence implied in the fact that the crucified and condemned is raised by God and vindicated. He returns as the judge of his judges. The court and city that condemned Jesus is still engaged in judging and condemning him as it confronts his church. And insofar as it continues to judge and condemn, it continues to invite the judgement of its victim, whom God has approved and exalted" (9).

victims of Paul's violence; he is those who Paul has oppressed, hurt, or killed.[41]

Once more Jesus is the victim of the powers, but this time through his body, the persecuted, suffering church. When Paul receives his call he is told that he, too, will stand before the powers in the way of Jesus.

> Ananias answered, "Lord, I have heard from many about this man, how much evil he has done to your saints in Jerusalem and here he has authority from the chief priests to bind all who invoke your name." But the Lord said to him, "Go for he is the instrument whom I have chosen to bring before Gentiles and kings and before the people of Israel. I myself will show him how much he must suffer for the sake of my name." (Acts 9:13–16)

Paul goes on to develop a theology of inverse power, based on the "foolishness" of a Messiah-king who was crucified.

> But we have this treasure in clay jars, so that it may be made clear that this extraordinary power belongs to God and does not come from us. We are afflicted in every way, but not crushed; perplexed but not driven to despair; persecuted but not forsaken, struck down but not destroyed; always carrying in the body the death of Jesus. (2 Cor 4:7–10)

The death and resurrection of Christ has not exempted the pilgrim people of God from the struggle of faith against the powers. Freedom will come in the fullness of time, when all things are gathered up into him (Eph 1:10). But in the ambiguity of the time in between Easter and its consummation, the church finds its being as it lives into the victim-sacrifice of Christ, knowing at the same time its capacity to be betrayer and perpetrator—a reality reinforced through its sustaining remembrance in the Lord's Supper. The sacrificing self-giving of Jesus is remembered with bread and wine, but only as that remembrance is framed in the recollection of complicity and failure, "on the night he was betrayed" (1 Cor 11:23). In identifying with the innocent victim oppressed by the powers, the church is not released into a righteousness that sees the oppressing power as "the other," for it can only identify with the victim-Christ when it has first acknowledged its own betrayals and complicity, its own part in the web of destructive untruth, self-deception, and distortions of power.[42]

---

41. Williams, *Resurrection*, 10–11.
42. Williams, *Resurrection*, 40–41. Williams points to the Eucharist, the church's

The biblical story provides an ongoing critical analysis of the working and distortions of power in human life. It consistently rejects the denial of power as much as its divinizing. It will not allow the people of God to escape responsibility for the distortions of power by projecting them onto the world outside. It is only with the self-knowledge of being betrayer, perpetrator, and at one with the victim that the church can find the integrity of its high vocation to show something of the wisdom of God to "the rulers and authorities in the heavenly places" (Eph 3:10).

---

recurring celebration of Easter as making memorial, not just of joyful table fellowship, "but the memory of false hope, betrayal and desertion, of a past in which ignorance and pride and the rejection of Jesus' account of his destiny in favour of power-fantasies of their own led the disciples into their most tragic failure, their indirect but real share in the ruin of their Lord" (39–40).

Chapter 4

INSTITUTIONS
Dwelling in the Grey Spaces

IN THE PREVIOUS CHAPTER we traced a thread of polarity and tension about power and "the powers" through the story of the people of God, where there is a recurring theme of faithfulness being worked out in the tension between power as a necessary provision and power as a risk and distortion in human community. A similar tension can be traced between the ongoing need for the people of God to adopt human organizational and institutional forms "like the nations" (1 Sam 8:5) and the possibility that these same expressions will compromise or corrupt the vocation of being a community under God. Faced with the temptation to adopt uncritically the structures of the world around it, or at the other extreme, to recoil from worldly structures into spiritual separation, the people of God are called to a more precarious way. They are to take the more uncertain track between the two, neither identifying fully with the visible and institutional, nor retreating from it, with both the extremes opening up a greater possibility of power being used coercively and even abusively.

"Like the nations," but called to account

The biblical narrative presents an ongoing and considered ambivalence about human institutions. Even when the providential nature of certain institutions is recognized, they continue to be subject to a theological caution and critique intended to hold them to their place under the rule of God. In Genesis the development of the institution of the "human city" enables a unity of human endeavor reaching to the skies, but at the same time it alienates people from their creator who then scatters them in a Babel of languages (Gen 11:1–9). Israel's move from being a tribal confederacy to the institution of a monarchy "like the nations" is accompanied by a prophetic warning about "the ways of the king that will reign over you"(1 Sam 8:10–22).[1] The Deuteronomic history looks back from the exile over the kings of Israel and sees the prophetic apprehension fulfilled; with few exceptions Israel has been repeatedly failed by the "abominations" of its monarchs so that exile is inevitable.[2] The Aaronic priesthood is established under Moses as a perpetual order, but almost immediately strays and incurs the fire of God (Lev 10:1–2). The king's desire to build a temple is initially resisted because of the risk that, in providing a sacralized focus for the presence of God, the sense of Yahweh's presence moving "among all the people of Israel" might be diminished (2 Sam 7:7). When it becomes self-serving, institutional prophecy finds itself critiqued from within by solitary figures like Ezekiel and Jeremiah (Ezek 13:1–7; Jer 23:9–40).

It is within this tradition of acceptance mixed with critique towards the institutions of the people of God, that Jesus seems to place himself as he approaches the city that represents them all:

> Yet today, tomorrow, and the next day I must be on my way, because it is impossible for a prophet to be killed outside of Jerusalem. Jerusalem, Jerusalem, the city that kills the prophets and stones those who are sent to it! How often have I desired to gather your children together as a hen gathers her brood under her wings, and you were not willing! See, your house is left to you. (Luke 13:31, 19:41)

---

1. Gaillardetz, *Ecclesiology for a Global Church*, 5. "Yet 1 Samuel reveals simmering political and theological tensions regarding this new development. Those in favour of the emerging monarchy sought to characterise it as a kind of 'limited kingship'. This new institution could be reconciled with early Yahwistic conceptions of community only insofar as the king served by the will of Yahweh and the assent of the people. Both these elements are dominant in the story of Saul's anointing by Samuel. Yet also imbedded in the narratives of 1 Samuel is another tradition that sees any form of monarchy as fundamentally at odds with a conception of community that submits exclusively to the kingship of God" (5).

2. See, for instance, 2 Kgs 21:10–15.

As Jesus formed a community around himself, it was as a movement of renewal and reform within the history and institutions of Israel, rather than in the establishment of something entirely new. To the extent that he proclaimed a new development, it was as realization of what was long expected, rather than a complete discontinuity with what had gone before. "I was sent only to the lost sheep of the house of Israel" (Matt 15:21–28). In calling a group of followers about himself, for whom the number twelve was significant, he is signaling the restoration of the twelve tribes of Israel. In sharing a meal in the context of Passover, he is placing himself thoroughly within the defining story of the people of God as expressed in institutional memory. In providing a prayer for his followers, he nurtures their belonging together with him in the acceptable way of Jewish rabbis (Luke 11:1–4). Rather than starting a new community or institution, Jesus interacts prophetically with the institutions of the people of God as they are in his time, reframing what has been, critiquing what is, and seeking to express what is still held in hope. The New Testament writers see Jesus not just as fulfilling the eschatological hope of the people of God, but also Israel's major institutions—the monarchy, priesthood, and prophecy—a theme taken up in Christian devotion down the ages:

> O Jesus, shepherd, guardian, friend,
> my Prophet, Priest, and King,
> my Lord, my Life, my Way, my End,
> accept the praise I bring.[3]

Fulfillment as continuity and critique

The notion of fulfillment, however, implies more than continuity with the past. Fulfillment is not mere continuance of what has gone before; it implies an element of critique and difference as well. It signals a something more, the arrival of something beyond what has been, that "someone greater is here" (Matt 12:41–42). While the notion of fulfillment affirms what has preceded it, insofar as it gathers it up, it also critiques what has gone before because it is a fuller expression of that which thereafter comes to be seen as at best anticipatory or partial. In Matthew, then, when Jesus claims that he has come to "fulfill the Law and the prophets," this great affirmation is

3. The hymn "How Sweet the Name of Jesus Sounds" was written by John Newton and published in 1779.

closely followed by a solemn repetition of the "something more" of fulfillment, "You have heard it said . . . but I say to you" (Matt 12:21, 27, 31, 33).[4] In John, when Jesus claims to be the "living bread which came down from heaven," it is not his claim to be in continuity with the past that causes affront, but the suggestion that something more had come. "Your ancestors ate the bread in the desert and died. This is the bread that comes down from heaven so that one may eat of it and not die" (John 6:49–50).

Luke uses the same phrase, "to be fulfilled," in a careful and programmatic way throughout his Gospel, but importantly then carries the same language into the Acts story of the early believers where he makes a careful distinction between "fulfillment" and "restoration." When the disciples ask the resurrected Lord if the Easter events mean that Israel's kingdom is then to be restored (Acts 1:6), he answers tangentially; the symbolic apostolic twelve is restored to its full number and the eschatological Spirit comes. National Israel will not be *restored* as it was, but it will be *fulfilled*.[5] In continuity there is also the tension of the different, the something more of fulfillment.

Just as the New Testament writers use the idea of fulfillment to capture the tension between continuity with, and critique of, what had gone before, so eschatology offers a critical distinction between the church in the reality of its human journey and what it is called to become. The vision of eschatological fulfillment always critiques the reality of the present, with its incompleteness, fragility, and failings. Through its eschatology, the community of believers knows itself as living in the incomplete; they are God's people now, but they are still called to "let yourself be built into a spiritual house, a holy priesthood" (1 Pet 2:4–10).

This eschatological ambivalence of "already" and "not yet" allows for both the recognition of what is and its critique through the vision of a better thing to come. As Paul puts it, the church inhabits the time between the "firstfruits" and full harvest and so it lives in the place of hopeful reception, but also of expectant groaning (Rom 5:1–5, 8:18–25). The structure of the Pauline epistles expresses this eschatological ambivalence that is the reality

---

4. There are sixty-eight quotations from the Old Testament in Matthew. The phrase "it is written" (in the perfect tense) occurs nine times, and a reference to "fulfillment" occurs twelve times.

5. Esler, *Community and Gospel in Luke-Acts*, 46–69. Looking at the theme of fulfillment in Luke-Acts, and drawing on the social theory of people like Ernst Troeltsch, Esler argues that the motif of fulfillment was part of the legitimation of a breakaway movement from its parent body. It conveys the double notion of continuity and discontinuity.

of the church, as Paul characteristically switches between the indicative and imperative, beginning in the indicative and affirming all that the faithful have already received in the coming of Christ and will receive in full with his return, then moving to the imperative and challenging the early believers with the "not yet" of their behavior, calling them to live into the reality that is already eschatologically theirs. So in one of his earlier writings, the First Letter to the Corinthians, Paul affirms that this infant church has been "sanctified," it has received grace "in every way," it has been enriched in "speech and knowledge," strengthened in the "testimony of Christ," so that it is not lacking in any "spiritual gift," and on the eschatological "day of our Lord Jesus," it will be found to be blameless.[6] This is the eschatological indicative. But there is more to say. Paul will not let the Corinthian believers comfort themselves in this place of spiritual idealism. He will not accept the arrogance of those who claim to "have it all" already (1 Cor. 4:8). He pulls them back from "already" to the "not yet," to the problematic earthly reality, shifting from the indicative to the imperative: "So now I appeal to you, brothers and sisters . . ."[7] He addresses their divisions, the arrogance and pretensions of their knowledge, the sexual immorality that mars the holiness into which they are called, and the abuses of fellowship in their worship. He challenges them where their spirituality has turned to arrogance, their speech has become the vehicle of self-importance rather than edification, and the exercise of spiritual gifts the basis of claims to superiority.[8]

The reality of the church is lived in the tension between its eschatological indicative and its earthly expression. It is holy. It is a community of sinners. It must sing "Gloria in Excelsis" and "Kyrie Eleison" at the same time. When it tries to exit this place of tension, it loses itself.

As we shall see, the tensions of Corinth were no isolated exception. Over the years similar tensions continue to surface whenever the church is tempted to deny the provisional "not yet" of its nature and make a claim to the "already," whether in the elevation of its earthly structures, or in claims of spiritual purity.

---

6. 1 Cor 1:2–9.
7. 1 Cor 1:10.
8. 1 Cor 1:11, 18–25; 2:1–13; 5:1–13; 11:17–28; 12–14.

Defending the mixture of wheat and weeds

Problems similar to those found in Corinth continued to emerge as the church grew and spread beyond its apostolic origins. As it spread "into all the world" it began to receive into its midst people from a wider range of backgrounds and circumstances, as it moved to engage more with, and even to accommodate, some of the cultural expressions and ways of the world around it. For some this represented a loss of apostolic purity and there were repeated attempts by groups like the Marcionites, Montanists, and Novationists to reimpose the more rigorous disciplines of earlier days. The main body of the church resisted these pressures, however, and the parable of the wheat and weeds became an informing ecclesiological image.[9]

One of the early conflicts that helped shape the church's emerging self-understanding was between Callistus and Hippolytus in the church of Rome. In 217, when Callistus became the bishop of Rome, he started to receive converts from sects or schisms who had not done a severe penance. He established the practice of absolution of all sins, including adultery and murder. Hippolytus, who was elected as a rival bishop in Rome, denounced the policy of Callistus in extending forgiveness of sins to cover sexual transgressions as disturbingly lax and criticized him for allowing highly placed believers to regularize their relationships with their own slaves by recognizing those relationships as valid marriages. In defense of his position, Callistus fought for an understanding of church that recognized it lived in the mixed place of the "not yet." He drew upon the parable of the wheat and weeds: "Let the tares grow along with the wheat." He also called upon the story of Noah's ark as an image of the church, in which all animals were gathered, both clean and unclean.[10] In the face of a rigorous ecclesial idealism—a push for purity—Callistus fought to maintain the tension between the church's call to holiness and its call to go into the world, embracing sinners, or to express it in credal language, between the two essential vocations of holiness and catholicity.

A similar debate later emerged between Augustine and the Donatists in North Africa. Donatism was prominent during the fourth and fifth centuries and, like Novationism during the third century, promoted a rigorist approach to the faith. The Donatists refused to accept that priests and

---

9. Hall, *Doctrine and Practice in the Early Church*, 239.

10. Hippolytus, "Refutation," 655. The position of Callistus is presented in a highly polemical way. It is significant, therefore, that his position held sway in the influential Roman church.

bishops who had been *traditores* during Diocletian's persecution could be fully restored through penance and that the sacraments celebrated by them were valid. As happened before, Augustine drew on an ecclesiological interpretation of the parable of the wheat and the weeds:

> You see tares among the wheat, you see evil Christians among the good; and you wish to root up the evil ones; be quiet, it is not the time of harvest. That time will come, may it only find you wheat! Why do you vex yourselves? . . . Beloved, even in these high seats there is both wheat, and tares, and among the laity there is wheat and tares. Let the good tolerate the bad; let the bad change themselves and imitate the good. Let us all, if it may be so, attain to God . . .[11]

For Augustine it was of the nature of the church that good and evil were always and necessarily mixed together during the earthly journey, mingled so closely as to make it often impossible to tell them apart. Good and evil were so thoroughly mixed in the church that judgment had to be left to God, and so even through painful conflict, he continued to call the Donatist clergy brothers.

Through these debates, the church journeyed into a wider space. However, the vision for a community of saints, justified, sanctified, and standing aloof from the world was never entirely abandoned. It found expression in various protest and ascetic movements, including the rise of monasticism, but because of these early debates this understanding no longer defined the whole. The church in its wholeness (catholicity) was a matter of wheat and weeds indistinguishably intermingled. The church affirmed an understanding of itself as a pilgrimage of sinners and saints, good and bad together, with final judgment suspended short of the eschaton.[12] It resisted retreat into a narrow spiritual rigor marked by the use of power to exclude.

Constantine and imperial institutions

Before long, the church was facing a temptation at the other end of the tensions in its being. Again the temptation was to identify the church in its earthly form too closely with its eschatological fulfilment. This time, however, the temptation came, not as the church inclined to retreat from

---

11. Augustine of Hippo, "On the Words of the Gospel, etc., where the Lord explaineth the parables of the sower," in Philip Schaff, *Nicene and Post-Nicene Fathers*, 6, Book 4.

12. Ployd, *Augustine, the Trinity, and the Church*, 53–55.

the world into the pursuit of holiness, but as it increasingly embraced the structures of the Roman Empire, with the risk of identifying the structures of that empire too much with the way of God on Earth.

Ruling from 306–337, Emperor Constantine gets much of the blame for this trend, so that while he is canonized in some parts of the church, he is regarded as perverter of the true faith in others.[13] Despite the drama of his conversion story before the Battle of Milvian Bridge in 312, however, there is evidence that the relationship between the church and the Roman world was already beginning to change. Some of it reflected a simple growth in numbers. By the beginning of the fourth century Christians probably represented about 10 percent of the empire's population and were widely spread.[14] The possession of sacred Scriptures, particularly in the more portable forms of codices, gave the church the potential to be "a world-wide textual community." What Brown calls the "basic modules" of Christianity had been established and were "remarkably stable and easy to transfer."[15]

> [A] bishop, a clergy, a congregation (called in Greek a *laos*, a "people": our word for "laity") and a place to worship. Such a structure could be subjected to many local variations, but in one form or another, it travelled well. It formed a basic "cell" which could be transferred to any region of the known world.

Some of the bishops had emerged as significant local leaders, and had influence in local government. Church buildings, albeit still relatively humble, were appearing. Before Constantine, then, the church was already moving into a place of greater prominence within the Roman world, engaging with the culture and structures of the empire, particularly at the local level.[16] Even if Constantine did not initiate this trend towards a greater

---

13. Constantine is celebrated as a saint in the Orthodox Church, while in some more conservative Protestant churches he is regarded as taking the church away from the purity of the message of Jesus and introducing many pagan customs into its life.

14. Part of that growth and spread was in the capacity of Christianity to gain a foothold in the major cities of the Roman Empire. To a large extent, the empire was held together through the links between its major cities. While earlier studies painted the first Christians as the poor and dispossessed, studies by scholars like Wayne Meeks and Rodney Stark have shown that in fact Christianity in the Roman Empire transitioned quite quickly to become a significant urban phenomenon. See Stark, *Rise of Christianity*, 129–40. Wayne Meeks developed this idea comprehensively in his book *First Urban Christians*.

15. Brown, *Rise of Western Christendom*, 14.

16. Brown, *Rise of Western Christendom*, 63–70. Christianity was penetrating all levels of Roman society. Marcia the influential concubine of Emperor Commodus was

rapprochement between the church and the Roman world, however, he certainly "turbo-charged" its progress.[17] In 313 Constantine and the co-emperor Licinius issued a decree that came to be known as the Edict of Milan. It assured Christians of the right to worship and also ordered the return of confiscated church property, while at the same time affirming the right of free and open observance by other religions. Even before this, Constantine had begun subsidizing the Catholic Church from public funds. This included handing over the Lateran Palace to the bishop of Rome, massively elevating the prestige of the church in the imperial city. Following the Edict of Milan, churches began to organize themselves into dioceses, along the lines of the local government structures of the Roman world. The bishops of major cities became significant public figures, and along with the clergy, received immunity from taxes and public service. Bishops were expected to act as judges and arbiters in cases between Christians and even involving non-Christians.

> As a result, the bishop, already regarded as the God-like judge of sin among believers, rapidly became the *ombudsman* of an entire community. Besides this, imperial supplies of food and clothing, granted to the clergy to distribute to the poor, turned the ferocious inward-looking care of fellow believers for each other, which had characterized the Christian churches of an earlier age, into something like a public welfare system, designed to alleviate, and to control, the urban poor as a whole.[18]

The clergy, with a strong grassroots network throughout the empire, increasingly became the people able to influence society from the bottom up. The bishops and a growing Christian aristocracy became increasingly influential within the empire's portals of power. The alliance of church and empire was demonstrated powerfully with the Council of Nicaea called, at least to a significant degree, because Constantine wanted the Catholic

---

a believer. There is evidence of a Christian "gentry" in Asia Minor. Around AD 300, a Council of Bishops at Elvira made a ruling concerning a number of matters concerning the local town council. The spread of membership also reflected itself in the almsgiving of the church. The fact that the church had so many in its care reflected the fact that some of its members were people of means, and produced a weight of local influence. Christians were known to look after their own.

17. Kaye, *Rise and Fall of the English Christendom*, 16. Kaye notes a suggestion by Rodney Stark that in some ways Constantine's conversion could be seen more as a "response to the massive exponential wave in progress, not as its cause" (16).

18. Brown, *Rise of Western Christendom*, 78.

Church to be an instrument of social cohesion across the far reaches of his reign. And among the bishops he made it clear he wanted team players. He presided at the gathering, paid all expenses, and entered the debate with the inevitably persuasive power that only an emperor can bring.[19] The unity of emperor and church displayed at Nicaea was enshrined in the new capital of Constantinople, commenced about the same time as the council and dedicated in 330. Built as a "Christian city," its architecture was lavish and the churches were given prominence of place. All this required a massive theological reframing, the tone of which can be ascertained in a lavish panegyric from Eusebius:[20]

> Again, that the Preserver of the universe orders the whole heaven and earth, and the celestial kingdom, consistently with his Father's will. Even so our emperor, whom he loves, by bringing those whom he rules on earth to the only begotten and saving Word, renders them fit subjects for his kingdom. And as He who is common saviour of mankind by his invisible and divine power as a good shepherd, drives far away from his flock, like savage beasts, those apostate beasts which once flew through the airy tracts above this earth and fastened onto the souls of men, so His friend, graced by his heavenly favour with victory over his foes, subdues and chastens the open enemies of the truth in accordance with the usages of war.

Finding itself almost surprisingly operating in close accord with the most powerful institution in the world at the time, the Catholic bishops were quick to take advantage of their new dimensions of power. With the complicity of imperial support, or at least intentional noninterference, pagan temples were violated, oracles shut down, statues of the gods beheaded and broken up, and public sacrifices were progressively forbidden. Church leaders who did not follow the still emerging Catholic line found themselves subject to not just ecclesial discipline but persecution from the emperor, who assumed the right to depose and punish bishops and proscribe their writing if he thought they did not comply with the orthodox line or his expectations of their behavior.[21]

---

19. Brown, *Rise of Western Christendom*, 61. Kaye, *Rise and Fall of the English Christendom*, 18–19.

20. Stevenson, *New Eusebius*, 391.

21. Stevenson, *New Eusebius*, 308–88.

Earlier, we suggested that when the church tried to resolve the tension of its being by focusing through its spiritual rigor on the purity of the world to come, the risk was that power became an instrument of exclusion and division. In the church that emerged under Constantine, there came a different set of risks for the use and abuse of power. Far from looking to set itself aside for the purity of the world to come, here we have a church that strongly identifies the presence of God with the earthly structures in which it finds itself as privileged, with an emperor who is "friend" of the divine logos, a world in which the unity of the church and the unity of the empire were intertwined, the enemies of the empire were increasingly seen as the enemies of faith, and vice-versa.

Not surprisingly, the risks of power associated with every powerful human institution came full into view as the church's newfound power was used readily and coercively to achieve compliance, to suppress diversity, and to punish dissent. These two ecclesiological emphases that we have begun to trace, with their associated risks for the distortion of power, continue to weave their way through the story of the people of God.

All mixed up

As bishop of Hippo, Augustine (354–430) lived with many of the trappings of a regional aristocrat within the Roman Empire. His church was not huge, seating about three hundred. He did, however, have the benefit of an extensive bishop's palace, a *secretariam* (audience room, where he would preside as a judge and arbitrate disputes), a warehouse to store goods for charitable distribution, and an impressive courtyard such as might be expected in front of the house of a noble or a palace. Moreover, when it came to dealing with his religious opponents, he was not at all averse to calling on the civil power of Rome.[22] For Augustine and the Catholic bishops of his time, the close relationship of church and empire offered almost unqualified benefits. Yet events transpired that prompted Augustine to invest some years reflecting on the relationship between the church of God and the earthly structures it inhabited. The prompting factor was the sack of Rome by the Visigoths in 410, which many Romans saw as punishment for the empire abandoning the traditional Roman religions in favor of Christianity.

Written over the years 413 to 426, *On the City of God against the Pagans* provided much more than an apologetic in response to the sack of

---

22. Brown, *Rise of Western Christendom*, 78, 91.

Rome, it developed into a massive exploration of the relationship between humanity in society and the kingdom of God. In *The City of God*, Augustine outlined his vision of two societies, that of the just, and that of the wicked, "the earthly city." Humans are social beings and human social entities (cities) are formed by two loves; the earthly by the love of self, which is ill-directed and contemptuous of true divinity, and the love of God, which is well-directed and of good will. From the fall of the angels until the end of time, these two cities and these two loves contend with each other.[23]

This approach might seem to be leading to a simple dualism, with the church identified as the "City of God" set among the evils of the "Earthly City." Augustine, however, avoids such oversimplification. The two cities are intermingled, as it were, "entangled together."[24] Although the state might be seen more a part of the earthly city than the divine, it serves the divine purpose and brings its own form of peace and benefit. The natural world, although it is passing away, does bear the image of the supreme Trinity. The church, although it might be seen as more a part of the divine city than the earthly, is subject to earthly pressures and politics. Those outside the church might be regarded as part of the earthly city, yet sometimes they show virtues that reflect the character of the divine city, whereas in the church, even among the leaders, there are those that are more tares than wheat.[25] Human society with its social institutions, including those of the state, are at their best when they encourage people to live in friendship and peace, but minimally they function to constrain evil.

Short of the eschaton, the church can neither claim entire possession of the city of God, nor can it set itself entirely apart from the earthly city. Even for those called into the heavenly city, the institutions of the earthly city bring order, protection, and a form of peace. All are part of the church's journey towards the new Jerusalem.[26] Augustine provided a substantial theological foundation for a church living in the tension of its being,

---

23. Augustine, *City of God*, Book 11, Chapters 1–7, Book 4, 1–7, Book 19, Chapter 17.

24. Augustine, *City of God*, Book 11, Chapter 1.

25. Augustine, *City of God*, Book 8 Chapter 9; Book 11 Chapters 1, 26; Book 13, Chapter 16; Book 14, Chapter 1; Book 20, Chapters 5, 9, and 10.

26. Augustine, *City of God*, Book 19, Chapter 17: "Even the heavenly city, therefore, while in its state of pilgrimage, avails itself of the peace of earth, and, so far as it can without injuring faith and godliness, desires and maintains a common agreement among men [sic] regarding the acquisition of the necessaries of life, and makes this earthly peace bear upon the peace of heaven."

between retreating out from the world and selling out to the world. The tensions, however, continued to emerge, often associated with contestation over power.

Crossing swords with power

Medieval theories of church and state usually involved the "two swords" model associated with Pope Gelasius (494), rather than the "two cities" of Augustine. Both "swords" came from God and had their own expressions of power. The church's sword ultimately was excommunication. The sword of the state was ultimately expressed in the power of execution. Pope Boniface VIII (*Unam Sanctum,* 1302) reshaped this doctrine, asserting that although temporal power was in the hands of kings and soldiers, it was to be exercised only as the church permitted, because things spiritual were superior to things temporal.

The Reformers rejected the claims of overarching papal power implicit in the way the doctrine of "two swords" had developed. Martin Luther's solution was a doctrine of two kingdoms, positing that God rules all things through two different relations, correlated to law and gospel. The kingdom of the law, or of the Old Adam, he said, operates through human reason and free will. The kingdom of grace, or the gospel, operates through the guidance of Scripture and the leading of the Holy Spirit.[27] Within this framework, Luther proposed multiple dualities: two realms (the spiritual realm and the earthly realm), two reigns (an invisible spiritual governing and a visible earthly governing), and two persons (the redeemed and the lost). For Luther, the gospel sustains the inner and spiritual life of the church, but does not impose any distinct external order. These outward forms are an application of natural law through human reason. In the gospel the church is characterized by pure equality in Christ, yet the church must have "hierarchy of stations" for outward order; "the rough and tumble of fallen creation requires hierarchy and differentiated order."[28]

Calvin applied the doctrine of the two kingdoms differently. While Luther was content to allow the state significant control in the external government of the church, Calvin came to the view that the external discipline of the church could not be handed over to the state.

---

27. Crouse, "Luther's 'Inward/Outward' Two Kingdoms," 1–34.
28. Crouse, "Luther's 'Inward/Outward' Two Kingdoms," 21–22, 32–34.

The Reformation in England had a different character once again, given that much of its impetus came from the state. However, the English Reformers did maintain a duality similar to that espoused by Luther, but tended to use the language of "visible" and "mystical."[29] In the sixteenth century, the Puritans emphasized the invisible nature of the church in rejecting the structures of crown and church maintained in the Elizabethan settlement and asserting that they were free to worship as they believed Scripture dictated. Richard Hooker tried to steer a middle way between the "conformists" who emphasized external authority, and the Puritans who emphasized the internal. Hooker denied that the visible and the mystical church could subsist independently of each other.[30] The church, according to Hooker, is a society "politic" (externally ordered) and a society "supernatural" (of divine origin). It is a "mystical" church, known only to God and at the same time it is a "visible" church that includes not just the "sound" but the "corrupted," including even those who are the "imps and limbs of Satan."[31]

Hooker's balancing of the "visible" and the "mystical" in his understanding of the church is carried through into his understanding of the relationship between what we now call "church and state"; although this is a differentiation that he probably would have found strange at the time. For Hooker, the church and state were coterminous, but distinct aspects of a Christian commonwealth bound together.[32] He attempts to wind back the prerogatives of the monarch, giving the crown supreme authority only in the outward governance of the church while denying any suggestion of earthly leaders having authority in the "secret, invisible and spiritual regiment" through which people are led to salvation.[33] In his commitment to

29. Avis, *Anglicanism and the Christian Church*, 8. As Avis points out, we need look no further than the Thirty-Nine Articles to see that the English Reformers affirmed the visible church: "The visible Church of God is a congregation of faithful men . . ." (Article 19). This clearly presumes an element of that which is "not visible, not open to human scrutiny, but remains transcendent or mystical" (8).

30. Littlejohn, *Peril and Promise of Christian Liberty*, 125–52.

31. Avis, *Anglicanism and the Christian Church*, 34–35. Hooker, *Lawes FLE*, IV.1:7; Vol. 1, 198. Controversially at the time, Hooker was of the view that the Roman Catholic Church was not excluded from the visible church.

32. Hooker, *Of the Laws of Ecclesiastical Polity*, 8:1.2–4, 129–32.

33. Avis, *Anglicanism and the Christian Church*, 48–49. Hooker, *Of the Laws of Ecclesiastical Polity*, 8:3.5, 154. "A gross error it is to think that regal power ought to serve for the good of the body and not for the soul, for men's temporal peace and not their eternal safety; as if God has ordained Kings for no other end but only to fat up men like hogs or

balance, he opposed absolutism in both the church and the state, and was an advocate of the principles of conciliarism: representation, constitutionality, and consent in both.

The precarious paradox

At a number of points in its history, as we have noted, the church has taken care to uphold a considered paradox in its self-understanding. This paradox has been developed in a range of complementary images and themes—the church on earth consists of wheat and tares, of two kingdoms earthly and heavenly. It may be described as visible and invisible, earthly and mystical. In each instance the conjunction *and* is significant. The church is indistinguishably wheat *and* tares. It is visible *and* invisible. It is intermingled *and* inseparable, until it is fulfilled in the eschaton. For all that it has a divine origin and ending, and is sustained by the grace of the Spirit, the church is also a human institution. In other words, the church has its place in the grey spaces of the in-between and there is no other sort of church on planet earth.

The rigorist movements we touched on earlier in this chapter emphasized the divine origin and holiness of the church at the risk of retreating into a narrow sect—a boot camp for spiritual athletes—rather than being like a hospital with doors wide open for the healing of damaged souls. Reacting to what they regarded as tyranny in the outward forms of religion, the Puritans so stressed the invisible working of God within the individual that the movement produced its own form of repressive tyranny, particularly when it gained political power, whether in England itself or in the American colonies.[34] On the other hand, when the church tries to resolve the tensions inherent to its journey on earth by identifying the kingdom of God too much with the human structures it has adopted, then the risk is that power will be used coercively to enforce compliance and to suppress dissent. One obvious example is the Inquisition.

---

see that they have their mash? Indeed, to lead men unto salvation by the hand of secret, invisible and ghostly regiment."

34. The Commonwealth and Cromwellian eras in English history (1649 to 1660) were known for fierce repression of Roman Catholics, but also Protestant sects such as the Quakers. The Puritan colonies in America equally were known for narrow morality and religious intolerance.

Idealizing the church

Similar to the risk of overidentifying the church with the structures of the world around it is the idealizing of its own institutional structures within. An example of this can be found in Roman Catholic ecclesiology through the period of the First Vatican Council and leading up to Vatican II (roughly the middle of the nineteenth century through to the middle of the twentieth century). This was a period of high church attendance throughout Europe and beyond. It was also a period of great change, with the rising influence of rationalism, liberalism, and materialism. The First Vatican Council was part of a reaction by the church to this changing world and it was characterized by an emphasis on the church as self-sufficient and unchanging. It was suspended before completing its business, having passed just two doctrinal constitutions, *Dei Filius* and *Pastor Aeterus*.[35] Nevertheless, something of the way the church saw itself in the world at the time can be seen in the material that informed the council. Patrick Granfield points to texts from the *Schemata* of the First Vatican Council as providing an insight into the ecclesiology of the era.[36]

> We believe that the Church of Christ is a perfect society. (*Supremi Pastoris*, 10)
>
> The Church is an assembly of the faithful of Christ, a true society, yet far holier than any human society. (*Tametsi Deus*, 2)

While the notion of "perfect" was used here in a quite qualified way, expressing the view that the church had all that it needed to fulfill its

---

35. *Dei Filius* dealt with the nature of Catholic faith, while *Pastor Aeternus* dealt with authority in the church, particularly papal primacy, infallibility, and jurisdiction.

36. Granfield, "Church as Societas Perfecta in the Schemata of Vatican I," 435–36. While the church could be called a "perfect" society, in that it had all it needed to fulfill its purpose, so could the state. Despite these qualifications, there is little doubt that the articulation of this doctrine was part of a theological idealization of the church in its institutional life on earth. The 1885 encyclical of Pope Leo XIII, *Immortale Dei*, provides another expression of this emphasis: "This society is made up of men, just as civil society is, and yet is supernatural and spiritual, on account of the end for which it was founded, and of the means by which it aims at attaining that end. Hence, it is distinguished and differs from civil society, and, what is of highest moment, it is a society chartered as of right divine, perfect in its nature and in its title, to possess in itself and by itself, through the will and loving kindness of its Founder, all needful provision for its maintenance and action. And just as the end at which the Church aims is by far the noblest of ends, so is its authority the most exalted of all authority, nor can it be looked upon as inferior to the civil power, or in any manner dependent upon it."

vocation, the linking of this language to church as *societas* meant that the outward, visible aspects of the church were idealized in what Granfield calls a "truncated and imperfect vision of the church." [37]

The church needs institutional expression, of course, but the idealizing of that historical and institutional expression, no matter how nuanced, has its risks. In his book *Models of the Church*, Avery Dulles suggests some of those risks. A church focused on its institutional expression tends to be self-important and triumphalist, "set in array against Satan and the powers of evil." It is inevitably hierarchical, with all power descending from the top, "while at the base faithful lay people play a passive role." It is coercive and juridicist, with authority exercised in a pattern analogous to the secular state, emphasizing the place of law and penalties. Spiritual ministries are not regarded as effective unless they conform to the prescriptions of canon law. Scholarship is expected to be an explication of current teaching rather than creative exploration.[38]

This idealization of the earthly and institutional aspects of the church provides opportunity for abuse and exploitation. Gerald Arbuckle suggests that it opens up what he calls "creeping infallibility" providing an "approved way for administrative, bureaucratic curial officers, bishops and priests to avoid having to be accountable for their actions to laity and to the church as a whole."[39] In the end, this idealizing of the church's earthly structures found in the Roman Catholic Church's pre-Vatican II ecclesiology, Arbuckle argues, still influences the church today, transferring the eschatological completeness towards which the church journeys back into its historical expression. Arbuckle is blunt about the effects of such an idealizing ecclesiology:

> Given the above description of the multiple cultural forces shaping the pre-Vatican II culture, it is little wonder that cover-up of the sexual abuse of minors by representatives of the church had become normalized.[40]

---

37. There were fifty-four references to the church as *societas* in *Supremi Pastoris*, much more than to any other image of the church.

38. Dulles, *Models of the Church*, 39. See also Arbuckle, *Abuse and Cover-Up*, 62.

39. Arbuckle, *Abuse and Cover-Up*, 62, 82.

40. Arbuckle, *Abuse and Cover-Up*, 83. Arbuckle draws on a group/grid model promulgated by Mary Douglas to characterize the pre-Vatican II Church as a "strong group/strong grid"—a culture necessary in some organizations, but which can be prone to "excessive cohesiveness" and no space for dissent; a necessary attribute perhaps in an army at war, but dangerous in a community called to the servant way of Jesus. See Douglas,

As we turn to Anglican Communion ecclesiology it becomes evident that there are risks of idealizing even in some of the more egalitarian models of church that have emerged since Vatican II. One of the most influential theological trends across most of the churches during this period has been the emergence of trinitarian ecclesiology, which looks to the sociality of the Holy Trinity as the model for human and ecclesial community. It is a compelling paradigm. The trinitarian God who is unity in diversity, complete mutuality in the three persons of Father, Son, and Holy Spirit, is seen as the pattern for human sociality, with the church called to model in the world a way of being that is a sign of God's plan for the whole of creation.

With the Anglican Communion deeply divided over issues such as the ordination of women, then wider issues of human sexuality, a series of international reports drew on a trinitarian ecclesiology as the theological platform from which to address the structural fractures that were emerging in worldwide Anglicanism. The 2003 *Windsor Report* is a prominent example. Commissioned in response to deep Anglican Communion divisions over the ordination of partnered same-sex clergy, and the church blessing of same-sex unions, *The Windsor Report* developed a largely structural response to communion stresses and the risk of division based on its trinitarian ecclesiology.

> Communion means that each church recognizes that the other belongs to the One, Holy, Catholic and Apostolic Church of Jesus Christ, and shares in the mission of the whole people of God. It involves practising a common liturgical tradition, and intending to listen, speak and act alongside one another in obedience to the gospel. In communion, each church acknowledges and respects the interdependence and autonomy of the other, putting the needs of the global fellowship before its own. Through such communion, each church is enabled to find completeness through its relations to the others, while fulfilling its own particular calling within its own cultural context.[41]

The application of such ecclesial idealizing to situations of conflict and disagreement within the church has its own subtle element of coercion. It confuses the aspirational with the actual, the *ought* of church with its *is*, the contingency and sinfulness of the church on pilgrimage with the wholeness of its eschatological completion. As powerful as the trinitarian

---

Natural Symbols, 57–71.

41. The Lambeth Commission on Communion, *The Windsor Report*, para. 49.

ecclesiological paradigm is, when it is applied to a church deep in disagreement and difference, it can have the effect of theologically suppressing the creativity of human conflict, not recognizing the "though-the-glass-darkly" nature of human knowing, and not giving adequate place to human brokenness. After all, it subtly suggests that if the church is to image on earth the perfect unity of the Holy Trinity, then deep disagreement and conflict can only be seen as a sign of unfaithfulness and failure. Such messaging always tends to favor the status quo and mute the disturbing voice of the prophetic.[42]

The church may confess that it is more than its earthly and visible forms, it may aspire, as it should, to the vision of unity found in the Holy Trinity, but it cannot idealize away the contingent reality of those earthly and visible forms, nor hope to avoid accountability when they fail.

> It may of course be irritating for the believing Christian to find that the church he believes in is unavoidably rooted in history, psychology and sociology, and therefore can be weighed up and compared with other institutions. The church he believes in can therefore, for all its desire to be something totally different, be considered on the same level as reputable or less reputable secular groups communities, societies and organizations.[43]

When the church idealizes its institutional life and structures, there is the risk that it will be unable to see anything other than its own theological cosmetics, becoming blind to the distortions within, the sin and frailty, the will to power and self-protection that are part of every human institution. Such idealizing can contribute to a culture in which accountability is limited and abuses are glossed over and protected.

Reifying church structures

Social entities are more than the sum total of people who belong to them. They are more than their aggregated parts. They have a dynamic of their

---

42. This is recognized in a report produced by the Inter-Anglican Theological and Doctrinal Commission (IATDC): "too close an identification of the doctrine of the church with that of God in Trinity idealizes institutional decisions made by particular ecclesial bodies. It runs the danger of confusing a theological *is* with an empirical *ought*. There is always a tendency for history to get lost in ideology, especially at times when the interpretation of a historical tradition is disputed." Inter-Anglican Theological and Doctrine Commission, *Summary Argument from the IATDC's Communion Study*.

43. Küng, *Church*, 35–37.

own. This in part explains why institutions tend to reify their own institutional order, that is, to treat their own structures and ways of going about things as if they are a part of the nature of things, the established or even the cosmic order, not just a product of human organization.[44] As citizens of a country, we routinely talk about "the state" as if it is something external to the people that together make up its population. We refer to the "law" as if it is an objective and powerful entity in its own right. A gathering of academics sitting in a room having a discussion over coffee might refer quite appropriately to the faculty as something objective and "other" even though every faculty member could be present at the time.[45]

In a way, this is human shorthand and it has some advantages. It gives recognition to the social dynamic of institutions and enables them to keep going through change and from one generation to another. However, there are disadvantages as well. Reified institutional habits and behaviors can be deeply resistant to critique and change. As part of what is experienced as a stable human landscape, they can be dismissive of criticism, intolerant of dissent, and blind to their own failings. Because the reified identity is so pervasive and prevailing, those within it can be blind to contrary realities, as institutional leaders in the church were, at least initially, in regard to the abuse of minors.

For religious institutions, reification presents particular problems.[46] Like all human institutions, the church tends to reify its organizational structures, rituals, offices of leadership, and the like. The difficulty here, of course, is that the church wants to affirm that there actually *are* elements of its life and ministry that are divinely inspired—for example, the sacraments of baptism and the holy communion.

---

44. Berger and Luckmann, *Social Construction of Reality*, 106–7.

45. That social entities can take on a dynamic and life more than the aggregated capacities or dispositions of members as history has been demonstrated sadly in Germany under Hitler, or heroically in the black civil rights movement under Martin Luther King Jr. Reification gives that "more than" of a seemingly objective reality.

46. Berger, *Sacred Canopy*, 180–85. In his classic volume, Berger suggests that the church should not try to avoid the sociological perspective, which will always tend to view religion and religious institutions as human projections. This is not to say that the projected meanings have no status beyond that of human projection. The social sciences are essentially agnostic of this. On the other hand the church should not hoist itself onto an "epistemologically safe platform . . . The contents of Christianity, like those of any other religious tradition, will have to be analysed as human projections, and the Christian theologian will have to come to terms with the obvious discomforts caused thereby" (184).

This appropriate affirmation by the church that there is more to its life than simply the earthly and institutional—that it has an inner, or as Hooker calls it, a "mystical" identity mixed with its earthly expressions—can flow through into the reification of the human so that what in other institutions might easily be recognized as little more than necessary human organization can develop an artificial aura of the divine. The symbols, architecture, and history that often surround what might otherwise be quite usual administrative functions in the church can give to those functions a gravity and power beyond their actual function. Survivors of abuse, for instance, trying to negotiate church administrative processes, even when the church is trying to be sympathetic, can struggle to overcome the sense of intimidation created by this dynamic. For those on the inside, as well, there is something seductive about this dynamic. For the clergy and other church leaders, it provides a sense of vocational affirmation and even power.

The challenge for the church is to ground its institutional life in realism and honesty, while it continues to "seek the things that are above" (Col 3:1). This should not be seen as somehow diminishing the vocation of the church, but better expressing its "wheat and tares" reality of being a pilgrim people.

Hubris, humus, and heavenly vision

In this chapter we have followed a thread of tension and ambiguity between the ongoing need for the people of God to adopt human organizational and institutional forms "like the nations" and the possibility that those very institutional forms will compromise or distort the very community they are meant to serve. For the church in the contingency of its pilgrim journey, the healthy place is in living the tension, "dwelling in the grey spaces." When the church tries to escape that precarious place by retreating into a narrow spiritual rigor, then the risk of power is that it becomes tyrannical and excluding. On the other hand, when the church overidentifies its earthly structures with the kingdom of God, then the risk is that power will be used coercively to enforce compliance and to suppress dissent.

As much as the church must be faithful to its divine origins and aspire to the perfection of its eschatological fullness, when it forgets its "wheat and weeds" reality and puts an idealizing halo over its earthly life and structures, it risks creating a culture of being beyond reproach, where cover-up and a lack of accountability can be normalized and the abused feel too intimidated to have their voice heard.

Sometimes the idealizing of church is expressed not so much in formularies or narrative, but in symbol and liturgy. In liturgical churches such as those of the Anglican Communion, where worship has been inspired to mirror the heavenly "beauty of holiness," the challenge might be to craft worship that more fully celebrates God's presence in the bread of human brokenness. This is a theme we will pursue in the following chapter as we look at symbols and liturgy as conveyers of cosmology and reflect on what they say about hierarchy and power.

Chapter 5

THE POWER OF SYMBOLS
—THE SYMBOLS OF POWER

It is Trinity Sunday and the bishop is present for the celebrations. The cathedral is near to full. The procession is assembling outside. The bell ringers are in fine form. There has been a full turnup of choristers and they look stunning, assembled in blue and white. Ahead of them, the crucifer and acolytes are ready. The pipe organ sounds a grand introduction and the procession begins. The choir, with the director of music, fill the aisle with solemnity and color.

The second procession follows on. The thurifer leads off, with the smell of incense and a rhythmic swing. Then crucifer and acolytes again, the boat boy, servers, master of ceremonies, and the cathedral clergy. The dean follows wearing a cope in white brocade, with golden orphreys. The deacon and subdeacon wear dalmatic and tunicle. The bishop follows in cope and golden miter, carrying a pastoral staff with worked gold and silver set with jewels. The bishop's chaplain walks behind in black and white with academic hood.

As the bishop's procession reaches the chancel, the organist augments the Great with horns and trumpet stops. In dignified order, members of the procession move to their places in the chancel. The bishop at last comes to the episcopal throne. It is about a third of the cathedral's length away from the pews in the nave and is ornately carved with a canopy above. The pastoral staff is put in its place near the throne.

When it comes to the gradual hymn, the choir lifts the congregational singing and the deacon comes to the bishop's throne and kneels. With miter on and pastoral staff in hand, the bishop blesses the deacon for the reading of the Gospel. The Gospel procession is accompanied by choral alleluias, and as the procession returns, the dean ascends the pulpit. It is a well-crafted sermon and the dean develops the theme of the Holy Trinity as mutuality in diversity. "Humans are made to live in mutual community, imaging the community of God the Trinity," she says. "All are equal; we dance the dance of life together. We are called, not to hierarchies and precedent, but to the gift of serving each other."

The sermon is inspiring and in many ways the liturgy captures the best of Anglicanism: dignified worship, a sense of the transcendent, the valuing of mind and art. But there is another message in the worship that day that has its own unspoken eloquence and it is a message contrary to the preacher's words and the natural dispositions of probably most involved. It is a message of distinction and precedence symbolized in architecture, dress, distance, and ceremony. The bishop processes next to last in recognition of Christ's injunction that leaders should be least and last. But the liturgical code is easily broken and everyone understands only too well that, despite the personal humility of the individual involved, the figure who comes in last wearing the golden headwear is the preeminent person in a parade of reverse significance. That the same person assumes an elevated position on a distant throne confirms the inescapable. The spaces, the distances, the varying degrees of elevation, have their own message and it is a message of hierarchy and precedence.[1]

Symbols and surroundings have a theological content and power all of their own that should not be dismissed. They portray a cosmology. Stephen Sykes once made the comment in regard to the dress of bishops, that "it is preferable to know who has the power to do what, by dressing them in purple and sticking funny hats on their heads, rather than having them slinking around the corridors anonymously in pale blouses and dark suits, casting votes in obscure communities."[2] While this comment by Sykes might have some validity, in that there is benefit in making power structures visible, the content of symbolism in worship is rarely trivial. When a

1. Lathrop, *Holy Ground*, 183: "Hierarchy is best known in practice. You know the list: The presider's chair looks like a throne, the entrance procession like the arrival of a monarch. These practices, even though they may be traditionally or anthropologically defended reflect a distortion of the Christian conception of church."

2. Sykes, *Power and Christian Theology*, 149.

bishop puts on a miter during the solemnities of worship, there would be few in the congregation who understood this liturgical action as some sort of "in-joke" of self-deprecating silliness. A sympathetic and informed perspective might see in that moment the humble assumption of the burden of authority, but what many will intuit, particularly those on the edge, will be the expression of a cosmology of hierarchy, with an ecclesiastical monarch putting on a crown.[3]

Church buildings, also, are far from theologically neutral. Church architecture is theology in built form. Traditional church buildings draw on an architectural pedigree going back to the Roman Empire and reflect the understandings of the cosmos and the church as those understandings evolved over the years. For much of that time, order was understood as essentially hierarchical, so that even in into the twentieth century, congregations could happily affirm a determined hierarchy as part of all the things "bright and beautiful" in the created order:

> The rich man in his castle,
> The poor man at his gate;
> God made them, high or lowly,
> And ordered their estate.[4]

Even beyond the intent of designers, buildings can be imbued with meaning by those who use them. Traditional church buildings in particular "iconize" a cosmology, a theological worldview that goes back to the Holy Roman Empire and is powerfully hierarchical in nature, with the movement towards atonement and the presence of God marked by graduated steps, increased elevation, and signifying spaces often carefully furnished for those whose separateness is marked by distinctive dress.

The modern liturgical movement has tried to soften these accents and reorientate liturgy away from graduated transcendence towards a more egalitarian expression; contemporary church buildings tend to reflect this trend, with the people closer to the altar or holy table and often seated in a

---

3. Lathrop, *Holy Ground*, 5. "If we know that human ritual almost always carries cosmological implications, ways that societies find themselves orientated to the universe, then what sort of 'cosmos', what sort of 'ordered world' does Christian liturgy imply? And if that cosmos is intentionally archaic, how can it have effect in Christian ethics? In short, is there a 'liturgical cosmology' that matters today?"

4. Mrs. Cecil Frances Alexander (1818–1895), who married a Church of Ireland clergyman who became bishop of Derry and archbishop of Armagh, wrote several well-known hymns, including the one that included this verse, "All Things Bright and Beautiful." In more recent times, this verse is often omitted.

semiround configuration. Even traditional buildings most often now have a nave or forward altar. But the artifacts of that earlier and hierarchical culture are rarely completely extinguished in Anglican worship, and for those who have been sensitized by the abuse of power, they can reinforce a sense of distinction and alienation.

It is important to remind ourselves at this point that symbolism and ceremony are not restricted to religious institutions. As we have suggested, among the distinguishing characteristics of institutions is longevity and part of the nature of all institutions is the way their identity is maintained over time through story and symbol, myth and ritual, within an encompassing story. In some institutions such as the judiciary, military, or education sector, these markers of identity can be highly formalized in dress, careful ceremony, and the use of time-seasoned symbols, but the more informal contexts such as when a family gathers around a birthday cake or shares the particular menu that, for them, represents a special occasion, are equally significant. In those countries where the protest march has over time become something of a democratic institution, what might appear to be the chaos of a demonstration so often follows its own almost liturgical formula, with familiar versicles and responses:

> What do we want?
> When do we want it?
> Now!

Where an institution is narrowly defined and able to exercise considerable control over its engagement with the wider world, it might be possible for it to maintain its symbols, rituals ,and narrative with little change and in close coherence over time; a closed religious order might be an example, as might an ancient and exclusive club, hereditary order, or remote tribe in Papua New Guinea. They are the rare exceptions. Most institutions in modern society experience the constant pressure of change. This is particularly so when an institution intentionally seeks a wide engagement with the world around it, though institutional change still tends to be gradual and evolutionary. As change does occur, however, the impact of that change on the complex dynamic of symbol, ritual, myth, and narrative can be uneven, mixed, muddling, and even discordant.

Symbol, ceremony, crisis, and change

On those rarer occasions where institutional change is forced suddenly—usually through crisis—there is the risk of the disjunction of narrative, sign, and ceremony. In Australia, the most significant ritual of military remembrance, and one of the country's most important national holidays, is Anzac Day (April 25), remembering the joint operation of Australian and New Zealand troops in the ill-fated World War I landing of allied troops at Gallipoli in the Dardanelles, as well as the sacrifices of defence force personnel in subsequent engagements over the decades.[5] A central part of ANZAC Day observances in Australia and New Zealand is a dawn service and march of ex-servicemen and women, not just in the major cities, but in towns and villages, to a war memorial where wreaths are laid and observances are conducted.

The COVID-19 crisis made most of the rituals of Anzac Day in 2020 and 2021 an impossibility. Australia and New Zealand were locked down, as were many countries around the world. In both countries, people were encouraged to light the front of their houses at dawn and stand on their front porches or driveways. It came to be called "Light Up the Dawn" and was widely supported on both sides of the Tasman Sea, accompanied by the haunting Last Post played by various means and often echoing from various directions all at once.

While the Anzac Day narrative remained largely unchanged, this reframing of observance had its own congruence and power. The experience of isolation that was part of the COVID-19 lockdown enabled a different approach to an enduring narrative and enhanced the aloneness of remembering and grief. Despite the changed symbolizing, there was a congruity of symbol, ritual, and narrative. This is a theme to which we will return.

The flood of mostly historic sexual abuse revelations that emerged in the Australian churches during the first decade of the twenty-first century also brought about a sense of crisis. As a board of inquiry established by the Anglican Diocese of Adelaide noted, the churches initially adopted a defensive narrative towards the allegations and claims that were emerging.[6] But in this example of change born out of crisis, a shift in public narrative was among the earlier responses, accentuated in some instances by key

---

5. ANZAC was originally an acronym for "Australian and New Zealand Army Corps," formed for combat during World War I.

6. Olsson and Chung, *Report of the Board of Inquiry*, Executive Summary.

changes in leadership and the introduction of new programs and structures for responding to abuse.[7]

Unlike the 2020 observance of Anzac Day under COVID-19, where the rituals and symbols were amended while the narrative remained substantially the same, with the sexual abuse crisis in the Anglican Church there was a shift in narrative, while many of the culture-enshrining symbols have tended to remain much the same. This was the point of our fabricated story about the celebration of Trinity Sunday, with which we began this chapter.

When symbols join the opposition

In every institution undergoing change there is the possibility that some symbols will become archaic. Where they previously supported institutional identity, they may appear as signs of resistance to new and emerging understandings. Architecture is an obvious example. Because architectural symbolism is so powerful and "set in stone," or at least in bricks and mortar, timber and steel, it can easily remain as a contrary sign as a new narrative emerges in response to change. But as that fabricated story of a cathedral feast day also suggests, beyond the physical environment of architecture, there can be other powerful signs in a contrary relationship to the formal narrative: dress, position, elevation, adornment, and gesture. Left as they are, these things can play a discordant background to a shifting narrative and they are all the more powerful because they tend to operate at the subconscious level, more felt than recognized, more assimilated than acknowledged.

These artifacts of ritual and symbol take us to the deeper levels of underlying culture and provide another way to approach the challenge set by the Australian royal commission: to look carefully at an underlying internal culture that, it suggests, contributes to the possibility of abuse and cover-up in the churches.[8] Where symbols or ceremonies are perceived to be part of an unhealthy culture, there is always the "neck and crop" approach to solving the problem, to minimize or do away with the ceremonial and symbolic altogether. The social scientists tell us that this is just about impossible.

---

7. The still painful change of public narrative was somewhat eased for the churches in that in many ways it involved the return to a deeper layer of narrative tradition, the identification of Jesus Christ himself with the most vulnerable and abused.

8. Commonwealth of Australia, *Royal Commission Final Report*, 28.

Human beings are symbol-makers and as Emile Durkheim's pioneering work pointed out, even the most ancient of human societies maintained identity and cohesion through ritual and symbol.[9] By way of chronological contrast, the twenty-first century advent of the smartphone and SMS texting was soon followed by the development of a range of emojis and memes, small pictorial symbols or images with their own informal conventions for use alongside words, but which can sometimes be used alone as the whole content of a significant digital communication.[10] One way or another, humans keep on doing symbols.

A defining Anglican debate: Hooker and the Puritans

Among Christians the debate about the value of rituals and symbols has been ongoing and sometimes deeply dividing. In the Anglican tradition it was given almost classical expression in the sixteenth-century debate between Richard Hooker and the Puritans.[11] In the view of conscientious objectors to the Elizabethan religious settlement such as Walter Travers and Thomas Cartwright, the Church of England was "corrupted with popish orders, rites, and ceremonies, banished out of certaine reformed Churches, whose example therein we ought to have followed."[12] In *An Admonition to Parliament* (1572), the Puritans made their case that rituals, ceremonies, and signs as retained in the Church of England had been so corrupted, that the "sinceritie and simplicitie" of the gospel had been abandoned and the

---

9. Durkheim, *Elementary Forms of Religious Life*, 166–68.

10. The COVID-19 crisis has provided another example of the remarkable way that humans can quickly develop and adopt symbols for their common life. When the pandemic began, the demands of infection control mandated not just measures such as isolation and mask-wearing, but also what quickly came to be termed social distancing. Various informal instructions and signs emerged to encourage or discourage people as required. At first these signs were improvised, ad hoc, and local, but quite quickly national and even international symbols began to emerge.

11. The Puritan Walter Travers was a reader at the temple and when the position of master became vacant he expected to be promoted. Elizabeth I and her advisors regarded him as too Calvinist and appointed Hooker in 1585. Steeped in the classical tradition while at the same time committed to moderate reform as it was needed, Hooker rejected the root and branch approach advocated by Travers and his supporters. It was famously said that at the temple, Canterbury was preached in the mornings and Geneva in the afternoons.

12. Hooker, *Lawes FLE*, IV.1; 271.

plain preaching of God's word lost in "popish remnants," both in "ceremonies and regiment" (worship and church order).[13]

Framed in his characteristically measured polemic, Hooker's response is powerfully ecclesiological, sacramental, and christological. Humans, says Hooker, are "sensible" creatures. He is not using the word "sensible" as we might today; rather he is saying that humans are physical, living in a physical universe, and apprehending that universe through physical and sensory means. For this reason, says Hooker, "sundry sensible means" are needed to move the human heart, not just speech as in the Puritan emphasis on the preaching. This, argues Hooker, is because the use of symbols and ceremony is natural to being human:

> We must not think but that there is some ground of reason even in nature, whereby it cometh to pass that no nation under heaven either doth or ever did suffer public actions which are of great weight whether they be civil and temporal or else spiritual and sacred, to pass without some visible solemnity: the very strangeness whereof and difference from that which is common, doth cause popular eyes to observe and mark the same.[14]

Hooker argues that human history had shown that words alone, as valued as they were by the Puritans, did not make such a strong impact as when they were accompanied by visible signs.

> Words, both because they are so common and do not so strongly move the fancy of man [sic], are for the most part but slightly heard: and therefore with singular wisdom it hath been provided, that the deeds of men which are made in the presence of witnesses should pass, not only with words, but also with sensible actions, the memory of which is far more easily durable than the memory of speech can be.[15]

Responding to the Puritan criticism that the simplicity of worship in New Testament times had been complicated with "means, innovations and devices" added over the years, Hooker argues that not everything is suited

---

13. Anonymous [John Field and Thomas Wilcox], *An admonition to Parliament*. This was a Puritan manifesto published anonymously, but widely attributed to John Field and Thomas Wilcox.

14. Hooker, *Richard Hooker: Ecclesiastical Polity*, IV.1.3; 122. See also Hooker, *Lawes FLE*, IV.1.3; Vol. 1, 273–74.

15. Hooker, *Richard Hooker: Ecclesiastical Polity*, IV.1.3; 123. See also: Hooker, *Lawes FLE*, IV.1.3; Vol. 1, 273–74.

to every age. While the "godliness of former times" should be honored, practices might be unfit for later times that were in "the first age convenient enough."[16] His argument that times and practices inevitably change is taken beyond mere pragmatism by a theme he develops throughout the *Lawes*: that the incarnation means that God is providentially present in history. Rowan Williams summarizes Hooker's theological understanding of history:

> The incarnation so associates God with the human condition in its frailty that humanity exhibits what Hooker calls the "effects" of divine action in itself... [H]aving taken an actual human body, the second person of the Trinity is forever united to a specific material thing which has endured a specific history.[17]

So while Hooker acknowledges the need for the removal of ceremonies that have been grossly corrupted, he resists the notion that something must be abandoned simply because it is in need of reform. Where practices or ceremonies have been subject to abuse, Hooker says, the answer is rarely found in the Puritan demand to be rid of them, for to do this is to run the risk of novelty and mere invention.

> Someone who wants to restore a diseased body to full health should not seek to bring it to a state of simple contrariety, but rather to a state of proper balance in opposition to those evils which need to be cured... [T]he first thing therefore in a skilful cure is the knowledge of the part affected, the next is of the evil that does affect it; the last is not only the kind but also of the measure of contrary things needed to remove it.[18]

In rejecting the Puritan argument that the only allowable worship practices are those that are expressly commanded in Scripture, Hooker makes a careful distinction between substantial matters such as the sacraments that are delivered by divine ordinance, and those lesser symbols and ceremonies "governed by human as well as divine ordinance."[19] These

---

16. Hooker, *Lawes FLE*, IV.2.3; Vol. 1, 278.

17. Williams, "Hooker the Theologian," 7. William Haugaard also comments on Hooker's use of history as a hermeneutical tool. "The other distinctive element of Hooker's hermeneutics was more exclusively a gift of the Renaissance: historical contextualisation." Haugaard, in *Lawes FLE*, "Books II, III & IV," Vol. 6, 157.

18. Hooker, *Richard Hooker: Ecclesiastical Polity,* IV.8.1; 124. See also Hooker, *Lawes FLE*, IV.8.1; Vol. 1, 298.

19. Hooker, *Richard Hooker on Anglican Faith and Worship,* 22. See also Hooker,

are to be evaluated, says Hooker, by reference not just to the principles of Scripture, but also antiquity and reason. In this context, Hooker develops three informing principles that we might summarize as *congruity, edification,* and *contextual diversity.*

Congruity

In whatever ceremonies or signs that a church retains or reforms, Hooker urges congruity between that which is signified and its "sensible" (outward) sign: "signs must resemble the thing that is signified."[20] Hooker is a person of his time and culture and his defense of the stateliness of Anglican worship based on a correlation between the worship of the church on earth and "the hidden dignity and glory wherewith the Church triumphant in heaven is adorned"[21] still leaves us with a hierarchical view of the church that some today might find challenging, notwithstanding Hooker's advocacy for a qualification of hierarchy both in church and state through the principle of conciliarity. For all that, the principle articulated by Hooker is an important one, that there should be an obvious congruity between a sign and the meaning attached to that sign, with that meaning expressed through natural association as well as any explicit narrative.

Edification

The notion of "edification" was an important one for the Puritans, reflecting the influence of the continental Reformation. Hooker adopts the language of his opponents here, differing from some of the conformists at this point by maintaining that the principle of edification needed to apply to those

---

Lawes FLE, V.4.3; Vol. 2, 31.

20. Hooker, *Richard Hooker: Ecclesiastical Polity,* V.6.2; 131. "That which inwardly each man should be, the Church outwardly ought to testify. And therefore the duties of our religion which are seen must be such as that affection which is unseen ought to be. Signs must resemble the things they signify. If religion bear the greatest sway in our hearts, our outward religious duties must shew it as far as the Church hath outward ability. Duties of religion performed by whole societies of men, ought to have in them according to our power a sensible excellency, correspondent to the majesty of him whom we worship." See also Hooker, *Richard Hooker on Anglican Faith and Worship,* 26–27; Hooker, *Lawes FLE,* V.6.2; Vol. 2, 33.

21. Hooker, *Richard Hooker: Ecclesiastical Polity,* V.6.2; 130–31. See also: Hooker, *Lawes FLE,* V.6.2; Vol. 2, 34.

things even where the church itself had power to determine things indifferent or "accessory." Where he differs from the Puritans, however, is that his emphasis is on edification of the church as a whole, with the determination of what is edifying resting with rightful authority, not just individual interpretation.[22] Following through on the principle of edification as Hooker articulates it, for rites, ceremonies, and symbols to edify the church as a whole implies a level of accessibility to the whole people of God, not just individuals, or sub-groupings. Where symbolism reinforces the sense or appearance of an "inner group" or clericalized elite, it runs afoul of the principle of edification as Hooker expounds it.

Contextual diversity

Responding to the Puritan criticism that the Church of England had neglected its duty to "frame her selfe unto the patterne of their example, that went before her in the work of reformation," Hooker agrees that in essential things the churches should seek to agree, and even in "things indifferent" he acknowledges that commonality is to be valued. But to impose uniformity across every Christian church in the "indifferent" matters of ceremonies, Hooker says is both "over-extreme and violent."[23] Across autonomous churches, "the state whereof is free and independent," with differences in geography, political environment, and culture, in matters of ceremony, churches should be left to their own discretion.[24]

Implicitly recognizing that different circumstances as well as the passage of time may mark distinct cultural contexts of worship, Hooker acknowledges that ceremonies in other churches may quite appropriately differ from those of the English Church.[25] This principle of contextual and chronological particularity provides a theological touchstone for the evaluation of rituals and ceremonies in a world of rapid change.

---

22. Hooker, *Lawes FLE*, IV.1.1; Vol. 1, 273. See also: Haugaard, in *Lawes FLE*, "Books II, III & IV," Vol. 6, 180.

23. Hooker, *Lawes FLE*, IV.13.1–5; Vol. 1, 327–29.

24. Hooker, *Lawes FLE*, IV.13.4; Vol. 1, 329.

25. Hooker, *Lawes FLE*, IV.13.8; Vol. 1, 332.

Same place—different worlds

Reflecting on the pace and nature of change in countries like Australia moving from the 1990s to a new millennium, the social commentator Hugh Mackay once suggested that all Australians had become like immigrants to a new land. If anything, his comments would seem even more applicable today.

> We have been plunged into a period of unprecedented social, cultural, political, economic and technological change, in which the Australian way of life is being radically redefined. Everything from the roles of men and women, through marriage and the family, to the structures of the labor market, the political process, the Constitution and the racial and cultural composition of our society is being questioned. Whether we realise it, or not, all Australians are becoming new Australians as we struggle partly to adapt to the changes going on around us, and partly to adapt them to our own liking.[26]

Mackay's comments about Australia could have been made about any number of countries in the Western world over the past half century. Even in countries where Christianity has been an abiding presence for the better part of two millennia, the church now finds itself trying to "sing the Lord's song" in a socially and culturally new and strange land, with shifting values and understandings of the world.[27] In a world where geographical loca-

---

26. Mackay, *Reinventing Australia*, 6.

27. We touched briefly in chapter 1 on Hugh Heclo's analysis of the shifts in Western consciousness that emerged from a range of powerful movements such as the Enlightenment, Romanticism, and Modernism. To these we must add the cultural effects of the technological revolution of the recent decades with what amounts to a new language of human communication, not just serving culture but in its own way influencing it. While culture has always been influenced by technical innovation (the wheel, the alphabet, the concept of zero), the sheer scale and rapidity of the digital revolution has produced its own cultural shock wave. The web-connected device in the home enables a different sense of space, time, and location for its users to that which was available in the pre-digital environment. The very immediacy of the digital world tends to reinforce the Western antipathy towards institutions characterized as they are by a long term view of things. Not only is the time horizon shortened, location is even less "local." People locate themselves within a network of digital "friends" that might be worldwide. The delineation between the home and work environment already beginning to be reshaped by technology has accelerated through the COVID-19 pandemic with the need for people to work from home. At the same time, the vast access to knowledge that the internet provides enables a selectivity that strengthens individualism; people can choose to learn what they want to learn. Across many local cultures and subcultures, a new "second" language is

tion for the churches may not have changed, but a lot of everything else has, Hooker's notion of contextual particularity, rooted in an incarnational theology of history, provides an important ecclesiological framework for churches to "re-receive" their own customs, symbols, and rituals with renewed cultural congruency and gospel relevance in light of their particular context. The geography might not have changed, but in most countries the cultural context will have changed massively.

Symbols, "Purity and Danger"

The anthropologist Mary Douglas wrote during the second half of the twentieth century, with influential works on human culture, religion, and symbols.[28] While she does not refer specifically to Richard Hooker, she does refer to the Reformation debates about rites and rituals. She draws a parallel between the anti-ritualism of ardent Protestants and the anti-ritualism of more modern times, suggesting such a rejection of "complex symbolic systems" can be seen as rooted in great social change, alienation from prevailing social values, and is viable only in the "early, unorganized stages of a new movement."[29]

> Then ritualism re-asserts itself around the new context of social relations. Fundamentalists who are not magical in their attitude to the Eucharist, become magical in their attitude to the Bible. Revolutionaries who strike for freedom of speech adopt repressive sanctions to prevent return to the Tower of Babel.[30]

Reflecting the influence of the early sociologist Durkheim, Douglas is clear that for humans some form of symbol making, communal ritualizing, is inevitable. If ritualizing is purged, it will rise from the dead. Attempts to reject ritual soon amount to the adoption of one set of symbols in place of the former. In this, like Hooker, Douglas sees a possible loss: "We arise

---

adopted both including and excluding and allowing new and different ways for people to access information and each other, and to use but also abuse those opportunities, as the emergence of cyberbullying among the young has shown.

28. The book *Purity and Danger*, by Mary Douglas, was regarded as one of the most significant nonfiction works of that era.
29. Douglas, *Natural Symbols*, 21.
30. Douglas, *Natural Symbols*, 21–22.

from the purging of the old rituals, simpler and poorer... There is a loss of articulation in the depth of past time."[31]

In rejecting the "load of history," the gifts of history can be lost as well. However, as social conditions change, the worldview (cosmology) and the way that worldview is represented symbolically will need to change also. It is not a "hard carapace" that a tortoise must carry unchanged forever, but rather it can grow gradually and change in response to the world around it. In a usage that corresponds well with the biblical understanding of *metanoia*, Douglas calls this change of worldview "conversion."[32] However, where social change is sudden and rapid, requiring a radical revision of worldview, then symbols can be left behind. Symbols can lose their meaning and rituals can seem dead. Even so, says Douglas, this more radical conversion will become in its own way a conversion towards "ritualist belief," one that gives meaning in the new social context (for churchgoers, often away from the church).[33]

Congruency and natural symbols

Richard Hooker was writing in a time of dramatic social change. The upheavals in and around the Reformation were far more than serious theological disputes. They involved great social and political shifts in the rise of the nation-state and its associated economic and military dispositions, the egalitarian effects of new technology in the printing press, and debates about how authority should work in community expressed in the conciliar movement. In short, the cosmological horizons were changing rapidly, and as Douglas points out, the greater the social change, the more radical the revision of cosmologies, the greater the denigration of symbol and ritual.[34] Such was the context of Richard Hooker's engagement with the Puritans about ceremony, symbol, and ritual.

31. Douglas, *Natural Symbols*, 22, 158.

32. Douglas, *Natural Symbols*, 158.

33. People can be drawn into different expressions of church on the basis that they are less liturgical, but often they find themselves encountering a liturgical and symbolic world that might be differently expressed, but not at all lacking in cultural power. The "Hillsong" movement, for instance, which began with one church in Sydney during the 1970s, has become a worldwide phenomenon that has its own symbolic culture and ritual forms, recognizable across a range of congregations, just as Anglican liturgy, for instance, with some local variations, has a basic shape and culture globally.

34. Douglas, *Natural Symbols*, 158–59.

As we have noted, Hooker's approach was to retain and reform, except in the cases where a symbol or ritual had become so grossly corrupt that it might lead to sin. In reforming rituals and symbols, Hooker articulated a policy that we have summarized as "congruity"—that what must be retained is some form of accessible association between a sign and what is signified. Hooker recognized that there was no simple formula for this congruity and he resisted the Puritan call for uniformity of ceremony and ritual because even in sixteenth-century Europe there was enough diversity of geography, language, politics, and culture to make such uniformity of symbols and meaning nearly impossible. In today's global environment with a cultural diversity well beyond the "learned and judicious" Mr. Hooker's known horizons, the challenge of developing or reforming symbols or ceremonies in ways that are widely accessible is that much more difficult. As anthropologists are fond of pointing out, a sign, signal, or gesture of friendship in one culture can represent an insult in another, and all the more so in a global environment.[35] Hooker's advocacy for commonality where possible, but local contextuality as needed, is, if anything, more cogent than ever.

In language not entirely dissimilar to that of Hooker, Douglas recognized the range of factors arrayed against the notion of a "cross-cultural, pan-human pattern of symbols."

> For one thing, each symbolic system develops autonomously according to its own rules. For another, cultural environments add their difference. For another, the social structures add a further range of variation.[36]

Nevertheless, Douglas pursues the "intuition" of some commonality. Accepting the proposition that human social relations provide the "prototype" for interpreting the relations between things, then "whenever this prototype falls into a common pattern, there should be something common to be discerned in the system of symbols used."[37] To put it simply, in

---

35. This can even happen across cultures that have great similarity. Just one small example: In some countries, two fingers held up in a "V," no matter which way the palm is facing, is understood to signify success and victory. In Australia if the two fingered V is held up with the back of the hand facing towards the other person, it is an extremely insulting gesture.
36. Douglas, *Natural Symbols*, xxxii.
37. Douglas, *Natural Symbols*, xxxiii.

the commonality of human experience we should not be surprised to find some widely shared symbols emerging.[38]

Body language

In *Purity and Danger*, Douglas explores social relationship and social boundaries through the matrix of that most common of human experiences: embodiment. The more deeply human bodily restrictions and cleanliness rules are explored, says Douglas, "the more it becomes obvious that we are studying symbolic systems." [39] Rituals of purity and bodily behavior are not just about personal boundaries, they are about social boundaries—about giving order to what sometimes presents as a disordered universe; or as she develops this theme in *Natural Symbols*, "the organic system provides an analogy of the social system which, other things being equal, is used in the same way and understood in the same way all over the world."[40] In the cultural glossolalia of the modern world, the human body provides at least one basis for a symbolic commonality. This is enhanced by the modern digital environment, where international applications such as Facebook and Instagram emphasize the visual as much as verbal commentary and at the same time provide the means to select and even "airbrush" images into the stereotypical and symbolic, as unrealistic as this might be. In a rapidly changing and culturally pluralist world, where the deposit of shared symbolic meaning is much reduced, body symbolism provides a commonality of symbolic language, notwithstanding some variations from culture to culture, as we have noted.

What is both encouraging and confronting here is that nearly all the primary Christian symbols and rites involve the human body. Baptism has washing of the body, the Eucharist has physical eating, confirmation and ordination the laying on of hands, marriage the joining of hands, and so it goes on. There is a rich and multilayered theology of body in the Christian tradition as well; the body is a temple for the Holy Spirit. The church is the body of Christ, and believers are baptized into that body and are called to offer their distinctive gifts as members of that body. There is a correlation

---

38. The "smiley" emoji is a powerful contemporary example of body symbolism.
39. Douglas, *Purity and Danger*, 47–53.
40. Douglas, *Natural Symbols*, xxxiii.

between ecclesial and sacramental bodies; "we who are many are one body in Christ, for we all share in the one bread."[41]

On the other hand, it is around abuse centered on the body that such an association of shame has developed for the churches in recent times. Even here, there is a sadly symbolic element that enlarges the trauma of abuse. Just as bodily movement, posture, and gesture in worship is about so much more than the body itself, so the sexual or physical abuse of a vulnerable other is never just about physical gratification, but power and boundaries. The abusive penetration of another's bodily boundaries has much of its long-term effect in what it symbolizes: invasion, conquest, and domination.[42]

So if the symbolic complexity of the modern world underlines the importance of body symbolism in giving expression to religious meaning, the sad history of abuse in many churches adds urgency to the task of reframing that symbolism informed by an understanding of body position, and power and as it has developed in more recent times. Elements of physical posture, proximity, movement, and ceremony that were considered edifying, or at least indifferent half a century ago, may well carry negative cultural baggage today. For the church to take seriously this changed cultural environment should not involve the jettisoning of symbolism, as the Puritans urged in their time, nor should it involve a simple defense of what is as it is. As rites and symbols are understood as both living memory and evolving understanding, the challenge is to return constantly to that question of the sign and the thing that is meant to be signified, at the same time being attentive to cultural factors that might take away from the central message.

We return to our imaginative cathedral service through the eyes of a non-churched twenty-first-century passerby whose curiosity is stirred just enough to slip into the back of the cathedral and watch the first few minutes of Trinity Sunday worship. Our visitor's eyes take in the scene: the long and colorful procession assembling, the towering columns and vaulted heights of the building, the distant sanctuary in filtered light, before returning to settle upon the figure of the bishop. Members of the church community know their bishop to be a humble person of genuine piety and simplicity of life, not perfect of course, but someone who tries to be a shepherd as a

---

41. 1 Cor 10:16–17; 12:12–26.

42. Sexual abuse always occurs in an asymmetrical power dynamic. To that extent, it is as much about power as sex. Motivation for the act is complex, as various studies have shown, but is often related to a need for dominance and control.

bishop should be. Our visitor does not know the bishop, as most of those assembled do, but is struck by the robes and golden headwear, the jewels in the staff he carries, and the regal nature of the whole proceeding.[43] The bishop ascends to a distant throne, and our visitor takes the opportunity to slip out of the cathedral back into the city streets. What image of church does our visitor take away from those moments? Most likely one of pretenses to preeminence.

Our cathedral story is, of course, something of a setup and intended to make a point. The experience that many have of the traditional church may well be more well-informed and reflect greater cultural connection. Yet the question posed by our story remains: setting all else aside, what did the signs of those few moments convey to our visitor about the nature of the church? What did the bodily presence, adornment, and movement of the bishop and others involved in those few observed minutes say about leadership in the church?

Rather than responding to these questions at this stage with a lengthy discussion of ecclesiastical dress and liturgical deportment, we allow them bring to us back to our discussion of the larger principle addressed by Richard Hooker: the congruity of sign and what is signified, along with the words that are spoken, within the particularity of a given cultural context.

Half a century ago in Australia, a procession such as we described in our imaginary cathedral service would have had more equivalents in the broader community. The use of processions was common in public occasions, whether it be at the level of national politics or a local civic ceremony in an outback town, at a university dinner, or a country high school assembly. Coming from a widely shared Western European cultural background, they almost always involved the recognition of some order of precedence.

---

43. I have intentionally portrayed the bishop here as male, although I have for decades been a supporter of the ordination of women. There are two reasons for this. The first is that the symbolic universe that still lingers in much church architecture and ceremony has powerful artifacts of the patriarchal worldview that prevailed in the church over much of its history and is still defended in some parts of the church as "creation order," not, as I suggested in the earlier examination of the primeval history in Genesis, a distortion of creation order. The other reason is that there is still a dominance of male leadership in many of the churches. The Australian Royal Commission suggested that the "absence or insufficient involvement of women in leadership positions and governance structures" in the some of the churches still negatively affects decision-making and accountability. Commonwealth of Australia, *Final Report*, 29.

This was mostly unquestioned as it reflected the worldview of the day and a shared cultural history.[44]

These sorts of processions are much rarer in Australia today, reserved for moments like university graduations or cathedral occasions. Yet in the nearby former territory of Australia, Papua New Guinea, the same sort of processions that were once part of Australian civic life remain still and often mark even the smallest village occasion. They are valued as very much congruent with Melanesian culture, whereas in modern Australia they have become more like cultural exceptions. So while there is undoubted cogency to the intuition by Mary Douglas that the human body provides a resource of common symbols, it is also clear that even these symbols can be read differently, not just from one place to another, but as cultures change over time.

One way to interrogate the relationship between a sign with what it symbolizes and its cultural context, is to ask two questions: first, in the terms of its cultural context, does this sign convey *in itself* something of what it is meant to signify? The second question is the reverse of the first: in this cultural context, does this sign convey something that contradicts or confuses the essence of what it is meant to signify?

Those who simply want to doggedly hold on to signs, ceremonies, or symbols without any change or development often argue that what is needed is nothing more than better instruction as to their meaning: "it's a matter of clearer explanation." While there is undoubted power in symbol and narrative supporting each other, Hooker's point about the relationship between sign and what is signified remains; there ought to be enough obvious connection to intuit at least something of what is signified in the sign itself. Where the cultural context has shifted, neither the abandoning of the symbolic, nor a dogged holding on to every detail of its set form, is likely to serve well. An approach that takes history and culture seriously will try to walk the incarnational way between these two extremes.

Again, we return to our imaginary cathedral occasion, seen through the eyes of a curious outsider. The physical movement of a liturgical procession is meant to mark a transition, to move those gathered from secular

---

44. It is generally recognized that the religious and secular processions of Western Europe, and those places that through colonial expansion inherited that culture, have the origin in the secular and religious processions of the Roman Empire. There is a commonality of the parade of precedence. Processions are just as deeply imbedded in South Asian and Chinese cultures, and are also full of color and ceremony, but they are less marked by a graduated precedence.

space to sacred space, to enable an entry of heart and mind into the "beauty of holiness." Can this be retained, but reworked in ways that do not also powerfully reinforce a cosmology of hierarchy and precedence that now jars in Western culture and reinforces the clericalism that the royal commission in Australia highlighted as possibly contributing to abuse?[45]

A cathedral is so called because it contains a *cathedra*, the teaching seat of the bishop who is also the shepherd, pastor, and servant-leader of a diocese. Can the symbols of the episcopate be retained, but reshaped to emphasize these essential elements of episcopal vocation, without at the same time signaling precedence and that same hierarchical cosmology? Can the symbols of the episcopate be realigned so that they speak more clearly into the world around them about shepherding and service and are less suggestive of monarchy?

Those who oppose or trivialize the call to evolve symbols and signs so as to be more culturally adjacent, and who suggest that it is enough to reframe the narrative used about them, are dismissing the very reason that symbols are used in the first place: they are powerful. They speak in their own right. As Hooker pointed out, they often make a more memorable impression than mere words.[46] For human communities, ancient and modern, symbols are deeply expressive of culture. For the church to take seriously issues of its own underlying culture, as it has been challenged to do in Australia by a royal commission, it cannot avoid looking carefully at its cultural symbols. As the church in every place and age receives its vocation to represent the way of Christ on earth, then it also must take seriously the way its symbols speak to its cultural context, to the world it is called to serve. Otherwise, it is just another institution talking to itself.

---

45. Gordon Lathrop (*Holy Ground*, 186–87) makes the point that leadership in worship is not the same as hierarchy in worship: "While leadership, even powerful leadership, is certainly needed in liturgical events, that leadership must always be subject to the breaking of symbols. Liturgical leadership must not become the focus of an ideology that weaves its assumed power into the essence of the church, let alone into the very structure of the universe. Every one of us—bishop and priest included—do not first of all participate in the liturgy 'according to our order'. We first of all participate, our hands out as beggars, with all beggars, for the sake of once again encountering mercy . . ."

46. Hooker, *Lawes FLE*, IV.1.3; Vol. 1, 274.

Re-placing symbols

There are various ways to realign the relationship between sign and culture. The United States has been engaged in a passionate debate about some of its national monuments and statues.[47] The more difficult debates surround memorials to the nation's founding fathers: people like George Washington, Thomas Jefferson, James Madison, and Patrick Henry, who were slaveholders and in some instances had businesses that benefited from the slave trade.[48] In a changed and changing cultural context, particularly following the death of George Floyd and the Black Lives Matter movement, these statues and monuments were denounced by many Americans as symbols of oppression. Some were defaced or removed, prompting then-President Trump to issue an executive order for their protection.[49] As an alternative to removing or replacing these now controversial symbols, there has been a trend to "re-place" them. That is, by putting them in a different place, or adding something else to the place where they are located, their message can be changed or at least nuanced without the sacrifice of history. Moving a statue into a museum changes the message. Placing a statue of a slave or black rights advocate alongside that of national leader who was also a slave owner also changes the message. Space and context change the message. Retaining a historic bishop's throne in a cathedral, while dedicating a new *cathedra* in a way that emphasizes a pastoral presiding among the people might be a powerful symbol, made all the more powerful by the fact that the old episcopal throne remains there and empty. History is thus acknowledged, as is the call of the people to God to make their pilgrim journey through history.

Reframing symbols

The "re-placing" of symbols is most effective when it is linked to a reframing narrative. In fact, the often made distinction between symbols and language is somewhat artificial. Language itself is a symbol system, expressive

---

47. To a lesser extent this is happening in Australia as well, particularly in regard to place names, where there is a strong move to replace colonial place names with their original aboriginal names, or at least to recognize the two together.

48. It is also suggested that eight of the first twelve presidents of the United States held slaves.

49. Executive Order 13933, June 26, 2020, "Protecting American Monuments, Memorials, and Statues and Combating Recent Criminal Violence."

of culture as well as capable of shaping culture.[50] The presumption, also often made, that somehow words offer greater precision than symbols is not necessarily true, or even helpful. Most translators of Scripture will be quick to point out that finding direct equivalence for words across language can be exceedingly different, because every language system is culturally laden and will have elements of its own internal logic that are hard to render into another system. In any event, when talking about God, the idea of equivalence in language presents great problems. All God language must be equivocal. "This" can never completely equal "that." God is love, but there is more to be said. God is good, but there is more to be said. The idea of "goodness" might say something about God, but cannot define God. As Augustine put it, when human contemplation offers a word of "likeness" about God, it must be paralleled by an awareness of the "unlikeness" of any understanding of God born of human knowledge.[51] So if we think of symbols as common things to which an element of ambiguity has been added, so "God talk" might draw on words commonly used, but to them as well an element of qualifying ambiguity must be added. Sign and narrative are both part of the human symbols system and are meant to dance together. When a rite, liturgy, or ceremony is reframed with symbol and narrative reinforcing each other, then both change and continuity are more likely.

Probably the best examples of this come in the institution of the sacraments of baptism and the Eucharist. Both were existing symbolic practices; baptism utilized in Judaism in the context of proselyte conversion, and the taking of bread and cups of wine in the Passover remembrance.

When Jesus gathered with his disciples in the Passover context of the Last Supper, his reframing words and actions brought new meaning to an already deeply profound story. Far from setting that sacred history aside, with just the simplest of actions and a bare few words, Jesus reorientated an already familiar sign around his own sacrifice and gave his disciples a way to remember not just his death and resurrection, but the saving story that preceded it.

When symbol and narrative are reframed together to speak more clearly and appropriately to their cultural context, not only is the "new"

---

50. Studies have shown, for instance, that language denoting gender not only gives expression to cultural attitudes in regard to men and women, but actually shapes attitudes. To that extent, language is not just a neutral system of communication, it provides a system or framework through which the world is apprehended and interpreted.

51. Augustine of Hippo, *The Trinity*, 15.22, 153.

more powerfully present, but so is the "old" more faithfully preserved in that it continues to function as living tradition.

Re-receiving symbols

In every generation, the church is called to "re-receive" its tradition, the gospel message. This is true of its symbols as well. Just as different emphases and interpretations characterize each generation's reception of the gospel message, so a contextual understanding of symbols and rites recognizes that faithfulness to their essence will mean flexibility in their expression. The liturgical reforms of the second half of the twentieth century reshaped important elements of liturgical symbolism in light of a developing theological understanding of the church as the people of God. The focus of the eucharistic celebration was shifted from the distant to the middle. The priest was shifted from "in between" to "among." The font was often moved from the door to the middle of the gathered people, reflecting a greater emphasis of church as fellowship of the baptized. These liturgical reforms reflected an ecclesiological shift, with the church being conceived as a fellowship (*koinonia*) imaging on earth the divine communion of the Holy Trinity. These theological shifts in turn reflected powerful movements in society towards an embrace of greater equality in diversity—the civil rights movements, advocacy for racial equality, the rise of feminism, and the movement against apartheid. However, the changes to liturgy and symbol were not just a matter of the church following social trends. A characteristic of the modern liturgical renewal was that in its reshaping of symbols, it sought to draw out to even greater prominence essential truths about that being liturgically represented. The notion of the Eucharist being a celebration of the whole people of God was no innovation, but the "re-receiving" of ancient truth for a changing world.

In the second half of the twentieth century, powerful social and ecclesiological movements prompted a creative shift in the church's symbol system through liturgical renewal. Widespread revelations in the early years of the twenty-first century of decades of the abuse of minors by church leaders has prompted further thinking about the nature of church and confronted the church's cosmology of hierarchy implicit in its cultural symbols. In some ways, the shifts in symbolism that were part of the liturgical reforms of the twentieth century were easier for the churches to receive, although "easier" should not be understood as "easy"; there most certainly was resistance and pastoral challenge. However, for the most part the changes were promoted from within the churches, could be seen as affirming of both priest and people, and as the church moving with its times.

Pastorally and practically, the challenge for the churches today to reframe what are important and much-loved symbols comes out of a more difficult place: out of the criticism of institutional failures, out of the criminality and shame of widespread abuse, and out of the community's critique of structures of hierarchy that lacked the accountability to protect the vulnerable. This is much more a call to *metanoia*, to repentance in its deepest sense of seeing the cosmos a different way. And it comes to the church from those outside, or from those inside whose voices are muted because they have been wounded. Yet out of the tragedy and shame of abuse there is the opportunity to "re-receive" and to express in liturgy the living tradition of Jesus who established the order of precedence in the kingdom of God, through the symbolic act of bringing a little child into the midst of his disciples as they argued about who came first, and who said of rulers who "lorded it over" people, "it shall not be so among you."[52]

---

52. Mark 9:36; 10:42–45.

Chapter 6

CLERICALISM
Playing the Insider Game

I SUFFER FROM WHAT some people call the "white coat syndrome." Whenever my general practitioner takes my blood pressure, it is unusually elevated. It's the whole aura of the doctor's office, including the uniforms at reception, the seating and décor, even the smell, which I hasten to add is not that unpleasant. But it has its effect so that the reading taken in the surgery is often not a very accurate indication of my day-to-day blood pressure. My GP and I have worked out a way forward. I take a set of readings at home over a number of days and bring them with me for a consultation. The white coat syndrome, if not avoided, is at least taken into account.

For the layperson, the world of medicine can be very intimidating. Doctors transport themselves through this mysterious world with an air of ease. As they do their hospital rounds they often have one or two white-robed acolytes in procession. They inhabit places into which access is granted only by some very distinct rituals involving something called the "waiting room," and they can have a tendency to speak in what can seem like very strange tongues. More up-to-date medicos, presenting themselves in slacks or chinos, work hard to break through the separating aura of their profession, taking great care to put their patients at ease and explaining things in accessible language. But the white coat syndrome often prevails.

For all that an encounter with the medical system can be slightly infantilizing, it can be the basis of confidence as well. This is because it has so many of the better characteristics of dealing with a social or knowledge elite. Such elites are not only unavoidable in modern society, but necessary to societal functioning. Elites emerge over time. As societies move from low levels of specialization, groups emerge with particular skills or perceived powers that gain them recognition and, in turn, status. On the basis of being perceived as having powers not available to ordinary people, they begin to be treated as a particular class. If the skills or knowledge they possess are seen as critical to the survival of that society, so their status is accordingly higher.

> Some people give evidence of the gift of healing, and societies recognize and give legitimacy to all sorts of healthcare practitioners, from witch-doctors to physicians. Others are skilled at making the fine distinctions required for prudential judgment concerning the balance between the common good and individual rights and interests, and society generates a legal elite. Others display wisdom in analyzing competing truth claims, and we get the scholarly guilds. Some know how to mobilize a society in order to defend itself from attack, and so the society begins to recognize public safety professionals and the military. And some are recognized for their ability to proclaim or articulate people's beliefs about the transcendent, or for their ability to lead the ritualization of those beliefs, and so we get priests, ministers, rabbis, imams, and shamans.[1]

The confidence that these social elites elicit springs from the skills and knowledge that they steward. A group or guild of specialists ensures that knowledge is retained, developed, and transmitted. Through a knowledge elite, learning can be advanced more broadly and quickly than through the pursuits of a gifted individual alone. In addition, there is an element of quality control. Most knowledge elites have a form of assessing entry and membership, whether through the apprenticeship system that came to the modern world from medieval craft guilds, or the granting of degrees and membership of professional associations. The person visiting a doctor who has displayed on the surgery wall, not just their degree qualifications, but certification of their membership of the college of general practitioners or the like, gains the reassurance that their practitioner is subject to peer accountability. They might be consulting an individual doctor, but can have

---

1. Wilson, *Clericalism*, 24.

the confidence that in some sense the medical profession as a whole is right there in the background.[2]

Alongside their benefits, all skill or power elites have their risks.[3] They can be excluding to those outside and coercive of those inside. They can be highly self-protective and secretive. Usually these negative traits are managed by internal and external means such as codes of conduct, rules, legislation, and, in some more hierarchical contexts, chains of command. When the checks and controls fail, the resulting damage is amplified by the fact that those who perpetrated the breach were part of a group recognized by society as having special skills, responsibilities, and status.[4]

By the broadest definition, most skill or knowledge elites could be regarded as "clerical," at least in the sense that the root word suggests: the allotment of a special skill or calling.[5] The focus of this chapter, however, is clericalism as it pertains to the ordained within the church. While the benefits of having a group of spiritual leaders are similar to those noted above as belonging to a knowledge elite more generally, it has been the negative aspects that have been brought to the fore in recent times, mostly though the exposure of widespread sexual abuse and the way church leaders have responded to it.

The Australian royal commission report identified clericalism as a major factor contributing to the abuse of children, particularly in traditional

---

2. Wilson, *Clericalism*, 27.

3. Arbuckle, *Abuse and Cover-Up*, 22. Arbuckle follows Michael Focault in making the point that there is always a coercive element in specialized disciplines: "Power is the pattern of texts, the specialised languages and networks of power relationships operating in a defined field. People who control specialised disciplines, for example, government officials, mass media moguls and religious leaders, hold extraordinary power in society, power that can rarely be questioned by outsiders."

4. The investigation of allegations of war crimes against some British and Australian SAS personnel serving in Afghanistan is perhaps a classic example. These elite troops are amongst the most skilled and best equipped. They are enculturated into an aggressive self-belief and are necessarily secretive. Because they are part of an elite, when individuals do step outside the boundaries, the ensuing results are tragic. In Australia, allegations against SAS personnel were subject to a defence force inquiry that produced what commonly became known as the Brereton Report.

5. The term originates in the Greek, κλητός (called) or κληρικός (an allotment or portion, initially of land). Thus today we might speak of someone with a "calling" to nursing, or academia, as well as the more common usage in the religious context. It is important to note, however, that the usage κληρος in the New Testament is not restricted to leadership elites, but to the shared vocation in the world of all the people of God.

denominations such as the Roman Catholic and Anglican churches.[6] Of the Anglican Church, the royal commission observed:[7]

> Aspects of clericalism—that is, the theological belief that the clergy are different to the laity—may have contributed to the occurrence of child sexual abuse in the Anglican Church and impeded appropriate responses to such abuse. A culture of clericalism may have discouraged survivors and others from reporting child sexual abuse, including to police.

And of the Roman Catholic Church:

> Clericalism caused some bishops and religious superiors to identify with perpetrators of child sexual abuse rather than victims and their families, and in some cases led to denial that clergy and religious were capable of child sexual abuse. It was the culture of clericalism that led bishops and religious superiors to attempt to avoid public scandal to protect the reputation of the Catholic Church and the status of the priesthood.[8]

As we have suggested, the development of some form of leadership elite is inevitable and even necessary in social institutions, including the church. It is what enables an informal movement to evolve from an ephemeral phenomenon into something that endures. It is part of what Max Weber called the "routinization of charisma," where the gifts of a new movement become institutionally imbedded and abuses of charisma are restrained.[9]

The benefits of the development of such an identified leadership cohort within the church are similar to those we noted more generally above. They can ensure discipline and provide a basis of confidence. The Anglican ordinal describes a candidate as being "called to the order of priests," so the ordained individual is called into the plurality of a peer accountability structure and is also subject to its discipline, hence the word "order."[10]

---

6. Commonwealth of Australia, *Royal Commission Final Report*, 32–43.

7. Commonwealth of Australia, *Royal Commission Final Report*, 33.

8. Commonwealth of Australia, *Royal Commission Final Report*, 43.

9. Weber, *Economy and Society*, 246–49. The *Didache*, probably written around the turn of the first century, provides an insight into this sort of process. It addresses the misuse of prophetic charisma for personal gain with some very specific and practical suggestions: "If he stays three days he is a false prophet. On departing, an apostle must not accept anything but sufficient food to carry him to his next lodging. If he asks for money he is a false prophet..." Richardson, *Early Christian Fathers*, 176.

10. Anglican Church of Australia, *Prayer Book for Australia*, 791. While quotations here are from the Australian ordinal, equivalents throughout the Anglican Communion

A recognized group of specialists is an effective mechanism for ensuring that knowledge is retained, developed, and transmitted. Once again, the ordinal affirms this as an essential function of those called to ordained ministry; they are to "study the Scriptures wholeheartedly," being "determined to instruct from these Scriptures the people committed to your care."[11] Generally, those who belong to a social leadership elite have been admitted through a process of training and evaluation, and again, the ordinal includes this provision: "They have been examined. Enquiries have been made among the people of God, especially among those concerned with their preparation, and we believe that these candidates are fit . . ."[12] Used in this general sense, a degree of clericalism in the church can be regarded as necessary and even beneficial. However, in more modern usage, the word "clericalism" is not such a neutral term.

The Australian royal commission report refers to clericalism as the theological belief that the clergy are different to the laity, with an idealization of the priesthood linked to "a sense of entitlement, superiority and exclusion, and abuse of power."[13] Clericalism understood in this way displays all the negative characteristics we have noted of other leadership elites; it can be excluding of those on the outside, coercive of those on the inside, secretive and highly self-protective, with all these general characteristics being amplified by a sense of divine authorization.

Theological props to clericalism

Even now, when people are described as having received a call by God, the common assumption is that they are heading towards ordination, the religious life, or missionary service. When people who offer themselves to clergy selection processes are advised that they should consider their vocation outside of ordination, they not uncommonly experience this as profound rejection and a devaluing of their desire to offer their best to God.

---

are similar.

11. Anglican Church of Australia, *Prayer Book for Australia*, 794.
12. Anglican Church of Australia, *Prayer Book for Australia*, 792.
13. Commonwealth of Australia, *Royal Commission Final Report*, 43: "Clericalism is at the centre of a tightly interconnected cluster of contributing factors. Clericalism is the idealisation of the priesthood, and by extension, the idealisation of the Catholic Church. Clericalism is linked to a sense of entitlement, superiority and exclusion, and abuse of power."

Some of these people are already offering invaluable service to the world with skills and attributes that should be the subject of the profoundest vocational affirmation. Yet the message they often receive from the church is that the most serious expression of vocation involves ordination. It is a distortion that not only panders towards clericalism, but turns the mission of the church in on itself.

In the New Testament, the word *laos* is never used to make a distinction between those within the community of faith, and the related term *laikos* (layperson, in the sense of "unlettered") simply does not appear. Nor is *klaeros* used to make a distinction within the *laos*, but most characteristically refers to the call of the whole people of God.[14] Even when it is not formalized, a theology of vocational distinctions sets up the possibility of distortions and abuse.[15]

Ordination and ontology

The royal commission identified the notion that at ordination a priest undergoes an ontological change and is thereafter "different to ordinary human beings and permanently a priest" as a "dangerous component of the culture of clericalism." Nearly all mainstream churches regard ordination as a vocation for life, but in the Western churches, there is a long tradition that emphasizes the permanence or "indelibility" of ordination. This was given classic expression by Thomas Aquinas, who spoke of holy orders as one of three sacraments that made "an indelible mark" on the soul of the recipient.[16] Despite some debate at the time, the Thomistic view became

---

14. While the term κλητός can be used in the New Testament of an individual, it is never in a way that suggests a distinction under God between that person and others within the household of faith. So when Paul addresses the church at Corinth he names his own gift and call, κλητὸς ἀπόστολος, and then goes on in his salutation to address the Corinthians in similar vein. In Christ they are κλητοῖς ἁγίοις σὺν πᾶσιν τοῖς ἐπικαλουμένοις το ὄνομα τοῦ κυρίου ἡμῶν Ἰησοῦ Χριστοῦ, "called to be saints along with all who call on the name of our Lord Jesus Christ." In the church, the qualification σὺν πᾶσιν, with all, applies to every expression of κλητός. Here a criticism might be offered of the ordinal in *A Prayer Book for Australia*. At the time of the laying on of hands, the prescribed words for the ordaining bishop are "Send down your Holy Spirit [on] . . . whom we set apart." A better expression of the priestly vocational σὺν πᾶσιν might perhaps be better expressed in a phrase such as "set among" (*Prayer Book for Australia*, 796).

15. Commonwealth of Australia, *Royal Commission Final Report*, 43.

16. Clark, *Aquinas Reader*, 488.

the standard in the Roman Catholic Church and is accepted by some of the streams of tradition within Anglicanism.[17]

Taking account of the influences of Aristotelian metaphysics reflected in the language Aquinas uses, this doctrine affirms that true vocation and call are not extrinsic to a person's being, but are expressive and indeed developmental of that person's being. To put it more crudely, true vocation can never be an "after-market accessory" in the human journey. The other significant point to make is that the assertion by Aquinas that ordination imprints the character of the ordained is linked in his thinking to the prior imprint of baptism and the Eucharist, sacraments for all the faithful.[18] Vocation for all God's people then, not just the ordained, is a matter of intrinsic being and development of the self rather than an extrinsic imposition. The call of God is always into a deeper experience of human selfhood and integration, rather than something externally imposed on that selfhood. Understood this way, the call to ministry in holy orders must always be entered as a journey into greater human wholeness, so an approach to vocation that stresses the ontological—that vocation is more about being than function—should provide little support for clericalizing distinctions. On the contrary, it underlines the call of the ordained to model that which is part of every vocation under God—the journey of being into greater human wholeness and personal integration of the sort that is denied in an act of abuse.

Apostolic succession

The notion of apostolic succession emerged in the church during the second century as a response to the claims of movements like Gnosticism. It was a time of doctrinal flux in the church and claims by Gnostics and

---

17. A relevant document here is a report produced by the Doctrine Commission of the Anglican Church of Australia, "Deposition from Holy Orders." Although the report's primary focus is on the nature of deposition from holy orders, it necessarily deals with the subject of the permanence of orders. This writer was one of the co-authors of the report.

18. Keenan, *Child Sexual Abuse and the Catholic Church*, 267. Mary Keenan points out the risk that an emphasis on ordination as personal ontological change, without at the same time imbedding that personal transformation in the experience of the community or the order as a whole, and more importantly of all the baptized. "In this theology of priesthood it is little wonder that priesthood is construed by clergy and laity alike as a personal gift . . ."

others to have secret knowledge or revelations posed a threat to the still emerging catholic church. In the face of these threats, the church took a number of steps to protect its apostolic heritage. The most significant was the delineation of the canon of Scripture. This occurred gradually, although by the close of the second century most of the writings that now make up the New Testament were regarded as authoritative. Debate continued about a smaller number of books through to the fourth century, but by 367 Athanasius of Alexandria was able to refer to a list of books the same as those presently accepted and used the word "canonized" in describing them.[19]

The doctrine of apostolic succession had a similar gestation period. Faced with competing claims, early believers were able to draw strength from the fact that in so many local communities there were the same Scriptures, regarded in the much the same way, similar expressions of leadership, worship, and catechesis and rites of initiation that had prevailed over the years. When a new movement made claims of superiority, or of having secret knowledge passed on from the apostles, the early Christians were able to point to the visible expression of continuity in these long-standing communities and their leaders. Clement of Rome, writing around 97 CE, drew on this principle of orderly continuity as he addressed divisions in the church at Corinth, with the apostles appointing bishops and deacons from their early converts, who would then follow on appointing "others of proper standing."[20]

Towards the end of the second century, Irenaeus wrote against the "slippery snakes" of Gnosticism who claimed to be recipients of a secret wisdom "not of this world" passed down by oral tradition. He appeals to "the tradition of the apostles, made clear in all the world," which he says can be "clearly seen in every church," with the continuity of those churches back through the bishops "who were established by the apostles." So, Irenaeus argues, if there was special knowledge that the apostles wanted to hand down, it would have been to these leaders to whom they were themselves entrusting the churches.[21]

---

19. κανονιζομενα (something being made into a measuring rod or rule), Arndt and Gingrich, *Greek-English Dictionary*, 403.

20. Richardson, *Early Christian Fathers*, 63.

21. Richardson, *Early Christian Fathers*, 372–73. Writing around the same time Tertullian takes a similar line in his *De Praescriptione Haereticorum*. He argues from the unity of the church and its continuity with its origins. All the churches, he says, "comprise the one primitive church, founded by the apostles," so that doctrine that which agrees with these apostolic churches must be considered faithful. Stevenson, *New Eusebius*, 177.

What becomes obvious from an examination of early writings about apostolic succession is that it is a notion that involves the interplay of several components: doctrinal faithfulness, the faithful continuity of churches, and the representation of that faithfulness in presbyter/bishops and later, as it emerged more distinctly, in the order of bishops.

This multifaceted approach to apostolic succession has been revisited in recent ecumenical dialogues, so that as William Henn notes, most theologians representing the Anglican, Lutheran, Orthodox, and Roman Catholic traditions would all reject the isolating of any one element as the sole means of establishing apostolic continuity.[22] However, during the nineteenth century both the Roman Catholic Church and influential parts of the Church of England adopted a more narrowly conceived view of apostolic succession, focusing on episcopal succession through the laying on of hands.

It was also a period of great change, with the rising influence of rationalism, liberalism, and materialism. Roman Catholic theology during this time tended to be reactive and characterized by an emphasis on the church as self-sufficient and unchanging. The language of apostolicity was "narrowly conceived as continuity in papal and episcopal succession and this continuity functioned as a *nota ecclesiae* (note of the church) in proving the legitimacy of the Roman Catholic Church."[23] For the most part, apostolic succession became defined by episcopal succession.[24]

---

22. Lutheran-Roman Catholic Commission on Unity, *Apostolicity of the Church*, 63. The commission acknowledges "forms of apostolic continuity, based on the books of the biblical canon, such as creedal formulas, catechisms, church orders, and common forms of worship, while not necessary in a strict sense for the gospel to be expressed with saving efficacy, are still needed in the church for its mission and its broader unity." See also Bouteneff and Falconer, *Episkopé and Episcopacy*, 61: "Faithfulness to the apostolic calling is carried out by more than one means of continuity. Apostolic succession is not the private possession of a bishop." Synods and councils are to be seen as another historic means of apostolic succession, so that the "bishop in synod" might be regarded as an extended instrument of apostolicity. See also Sullivan, *From Apostles to Bishops*, 235: "one can not only begin to draw a judgement about the ministry in a community and draw conclusions about its ecclesial character; one can also begin with a judgement about its ecclesial character and draw conclusions about its ministry."

23. Lutheran-Roman Catholic Commission on Unity, *Apostolicity of the Church*, 68.

24. This was well illustrated with the debate about Anglican orders, with Pope Leo's *Apostolicae Curae* focused almost entirely on the act of ordination. Vatican II effected a rebalancing, whereby the notion of episcopal succession was articulated more in terms of the faithfulness of the whole episcopal college, and the apostolicity of the ordained reconnected to that of the whole people of God.

The English Church during the nineteenth century also found itself reacting to a changing world. Moves towards the toleration of dissent and the beginnings of denominational pluralism were seen by some as undermining the theological foundations of the established church.[25] If the Erastian paradigm supporting Anglicanism was seen to be failing, then a new paradigm of authority was needed. For one influential group of leaders of what came to be known as the Oxford Movement, the answer lay in the apostolic succession of bishops. This emphasis of the Oxford Movement was given clear expression in Newman's Tract 1. There apostolic succession was couched in the terms of the "power of ordination," passed down as a sacred gift from "hand to hand."[26]

While more recent ecclesiology in both the Roman Catholic and Anglican churches has returned to a more multifaceted approach to apostolic succession, the cultural legacy of these nineteenth-century emphases lingers on. Often operating at an informal level, it supports a sense of separate clerical vocation and ontological difference at the expense of the laity.

> It is crucial to understand that the assertion required to focus and establish identity is not an act perpetrated in a vacuum. On the contrary, it is an act perpetrated against another. In re-establishing its threatened identity in the face of secularism the Anglican (and

---

25. Following the passing of the Catholic Emancipation Act 1829, Roman Catholics had taken seats in the Parliament of Westminster. The Reform Acts of 1832 were seen as further threatening the political hegemony of the Church of England. Chadwick, *Spirit of the Oxford Movement*, 3: "If the government, which has for so long given privileges and fetters, seems to be at last neutral amidst the religious divisions of Ireland; if the government seems to lay rough hands upon ancient church endowments without consulting . . . if the government must henceforth take serious account of the demands, or even prejudices of non-Anglicans in the House of Commons—then it is time to assert that nevertheless the Church of England has a claim upon the allegiance of Englishmen . . . because this church is teaching catholic truth."

26. John Henry Newman, *Tracts for the Times*, Tract 1, 11: "We have been born, not of blood, nor of the will of the flesh, nor of the will of man, but of God. The Lord Jesus Christ gave his Spirit to His Apostles; they in turn laid their hands on those who should succeed them; and these again on others; and so the sacred gift has been handed down to our present Bishops, who have appointed us as their assistants, and in some sense representatives. Has he any right, except as having received the power from those who consecrated him to be a Bishop? He could not give what he had never received. It is plain then that he but transmits; and that the Christian Ministry is a succession. And if we trace back the power of ordination from hand to hand, of course we shall come to the Apostles at last. We know we do, as a plain historical fact: and therefore all we, who have been ordained Clergy, in the very form of our ordination acknowledged the doctrine of the Apostolical Succession."

here I mean the most theologically self-assertive catholic wing of Anglicanism) ordained hierarchy came to conceive itself by means of an identity which, in asserting itself, correspondingly denied identity to the other, that is, the laity.[27]

Whereas in its earliest expressions, the idea of apostolic succession bound congregations and leaders together in accountability to their apostolic heritage, a distortion of this doctrine can feed a culture of "in-house" clerical accountability, which with a sprinkling of the inevitable tendency towards self-protection can lean towards very little accountability at all.

Cultural and symbolic props of clericalism

The theology of clericalism is often expressed and reinforced informally, in the daily habits of clergy and congregations, of bishops and dioceses.[28] For this reason it is often uncritically accepted as part of the scenery, and is therefore all the more powerful.

My susceptibility to "white coat syndrome" is an example of how an informal "working culture" can have a subconscious effect quite different to what is consciously intended. My GP, as it turns out, is nearly young enough to be my son, often wears jeans to work, and just occasionally calls me "mate" as Australians are wont to do. The last thing he would want to do was to create anxiety in one of his patients. Attending an appointment, I understand all that. The logic is persuasive, but not persuasive enough for the sphygmomanometer. There is something deeper, more complex going on. This is the complexity and power of culture. It defies simple definition and easy unpicking. It is there in the formal, but most often hides in the informal.[29]

---

27. Roberts, "Lord, Bondsman and Churchman," 161.

28. Arbuckle, *Abuse and Cover-Up*, 18, quotes Pope Francis in talking about the "culture unconscious." Culture is all the more powerful when is simply part of the accepted scenery. George Wilson put it like this: "Not only is much of the reality informal and (only apparently) trivial and transitory, but also the actual workings of a culture, its operating dynamics, are largely unconscious, not easily accessible even to those who live it out each day of their lives." *Clericalism*, 19.

29. Geertz, *The Interpretation of Cultures*, 5. The complexity of culture is illustrated by the multiplicity of definitions offered to describe it. Geertz goes on to make the point that a systematic theory of culture is almost impossible, or if it is attempted inadequate, because "stated independently of their applications, they seem either commonplace or vacant." Culture is not only complex, it is contextual.

Whether it be in the medical profession, academia, or the church, the cultural complex of social or professional elites involves formal and informal symbols, titles, special language, and even specifically reserved spaces (whether in the church sanctuary or the company car park). Like all cultural indicators, they are apprehended at different levels including the unconscious and are subject to shifts of significance.[30] The clerical collar worn downtown on a day when sexual abuse within the church is in the headlines will almost certainly produce a different response than it might have several decades ago, when clergy were amongst the most trusted of figures.

The culture that those in ordained ministry share has all the illusiveness, complexity, and contextuality of any specialist or professional elite. Part of the call to *metanoia* that has come to the church through the shame of abuse is to discern afresh those elements of culture among the ordained that appropriately express vocation, as opposed to those other elements that simply reinforce clericalism. While some practices and habits might be seen as relatively harmless by those inside the system, a gospel perspective would suggest that the principle of the outsider ought to inform all considerations:

> If any of you put a stumbling block before one of these little ones who believe in me, it would be better for you if a great millstone were fastened around your neck and you were drowned in the depth of the sea. (Matt 18:6)

Here a veritable litany of questions arise, some of which might seem of little note, but have their power in contributing to an overall effect, reinforcing the wrong sort of clerical "otherness." Is it time, for instance, to set

---

30. Cultural symbols might be thought of as operating at three significant levels; the general, the contextual, and the individual. They have to be understood in generality, or they have no significance. The police officer's uniform will not serve its purpose unless its significance is generally understood. However, with police in Australia having a follow-up role in support of COVID-19 protective measures, it quickly became evident that for some refugee communities that very same uniform conveyed a far more frightening significance than it might have for the bulk of the population. For many from a refugee background, the sight of a uniform carried the significance of a past, where all too often law enforcement agencies had been instruments of oppression. Cultural symbols come to us contextually, just as they also come individually. Returning to my "white coat syndrome," I might comfort myself that I am not entirely alone in my response to the symbols of the medical profession, but the fact is that there are plenty of people who are not so troubled. The complexity of factors that trigger my reaction are part of my personal history, and probably those of my family.

aside the titles and dress of precedence among clergy on all but the rarest and most ceremonial of occasions? In a church increasingly at the edge in Western countries like Australia, could the imaging of Jesus through the people of God be better served if bishops set aside the customary use of "Right" and "Most," and senior priests no longer aspired to be "Venerable"? Distinctive dress serves its purpose in many professions, and in the church clerical dress should remind the wearers that they act not out of their own capacities or inclinations, but are called to "put on Christ," linking themselves symbolically with the act of God in time and history that we call incarnation. That link, as well as the bond between clergy in their call of common service, would surely be more powerfully expressed in simplicity and commonality, with minimal distinctions, in contrast to the peacock parade of precedence that can sometimes mark major occasions, at least in the Anglican context.[31]

Clergy conditions of service can also reinforce a sense of clerical difference. The idea of a benefice and a living is a product of the patronage systems of preindustrial Europe.[32] At its best it maintains a system where clergy are provided sufficient to live on, freed from the anxieties of "house and hearth," and are enabled to pursue their ministry. The unintended consequence of these arrangements is that clergy members can feel disempowered in the management of their lives and can sometimes be drawn into the pursuit of a "plum" parish or preferment in the absence of more transparent processes of recognition and affirmation.[33]

---

31. The possibility should be at least considered that as clergy status has declined in recent years, there is a tendency to hold even more tightly to the affirmation of titles and symbols of precedence.

32. Max Weber's analysis of what he calls "Patrimonial Maintenance" still has remarkable applicability to the conditions of appointment and service for Anglican clergy in many countries, particularly where that country has had a history as part of the British Empire. See *Economy and Society*, 235–36. Weber is famous for his characterization of three forms of organizational authority and their associated leadership expressions. His characterization of "traditional authority" still resonated with much in structures of authority and power within the traditional churches, including those of the Anglican Communion. It is strongly based on personal loyalty, even at times over "impersonal duty." Accordingly, it operates through patronage and favor and is supported by the granting of a "living" from the master's table as part of a benefice, which often included use of land (a glebe) or housing. *Economy and Society*, 227–41. Among a privileged elite, it can lead to cronyism and mutual protectionism.

33. Another unintended consequence, at least in Australia, is that clergy do not stay long in parishes. In Australia over recent years, the average incumbency in the Anglican Church of Australia has been about four years, while all the evidence suggests that this is

While the provision of housing or additional allowances are made within several professions for appointments to more remote areas, there is an argument to suggest that such provisions add little to the mission of the church in urban parts of countries like Australia, and in fact reinforce the sense of clerical separation. Surely a priest who has to struggle with rent or a mortgage as others do, and whose salary system parallels others at an appropriate level in society, with increments through a transparent and accessible system, is more at one with the people he or she is called to serve than under the differentiating system that presently prevails in Australia and most other provinces of the Anglican Communion.[34]

These are just a few examples of long-established practices that half a century ago would have been upheld without question and even today, on their own, might be seen as of little consequence. To regard them in isolation, however, is to fail to appreciate the complex nature of culture, made up as it is by countless small things that together have power to hurt or to heal well beyond the sum of their parts.[35] Together they interact in the chemistry of clericalism.

Adrian Maclean makes the point that cultural change will be ineffective if it only addresses what he calls the "high-profile" level. It is in close attention to the many "low-profile" factors that a shift of culture becomes possible. To put this in the language of ecclesiology, it is not just that which is formally articulated that must be taken into consideration, but the "working ecclesiology" of organizational habits, the taken for granted—that which is regarded as background or simply unrecognized.[36] Jesus had a disconcerting habit of putting his finger on just such things: the fringes and

---

too short for pastoral effectiveness.

34. I confess I have changed my mind on this subject. As a diocesan bishop I supported the traditional system of stipend, housing, and allowances, largely because of its tax efficiency. My thinking changed as I worked to see the church more through the eyes of the outsiders and abused, and as I reflected further on the missional imperatives of the church in a secular and pluralist society. Even at the cost of losing some financial advantages for parishes and clergy, it is important that the church be seen to eschew its long-held presumptions of privilege.

35. Arbuckle, *Abuse and Cover-Up*, 9.

36. McLean, *Leadership and Cultural Webs in Organisations*, 51. "This is what we mean by low-profile symbols. They are the seemingly irrelevant and mundane everyday phenomenon that form part of the pervasive culture of organizational life. A context so familiar as to be taken for granted and considered normal. Low-profile symbols are like water to fish." Ecclesiologically speaking, they are the day-to-day life habits of a community of faith. See also Driver, *Polity of Persuasion*, 7.

phylacteries of the pharisaic culture, the cultivation of public salutations and titles by the religious elite, the attentiveness to the order of seating and the addiction to precision, even in the tithing of herbs (Matt 23:5, 7, 23; Luke 14:7–11). He was not engaging in trivial criticism. He understood how culture revealed the unacknowledged "big stuff" through the almost mundane and taken for granted.[37]

Changing the game: playing together

It is tempting to see clericalism as a problem of the clergy. If anything, such a perspective reinforces the problem. Clericalism, like any other culture, is "generated and maintained by everyone in the system."[38]

> Like any other culture, the clerical culture is the product of everyone affected by—or implicated in—its continuance. That includes equally those who are seen as laypeople vis-à-vis a particular body of clergy. Cultures are generated by the behavioural interactions between a particular clergy and its corresponding laity. The generation and continuance of a culture is a matter of relationships, a single reality mutually created by both sets of participants.

A change to the church's clerical culture requires, as much as anything else, an adult assertiveness from the laity, if for no other reason than that history demonstrates that elites who hold power are inevitably reluctant to surrender it. In the end, as Paul Lakeland points out, adult maturity is always something achieved rather than granted. It is there to be recognized and celebrated by others, but cannot simply be bestowed by another.

> The principal reason why it is a lay responsibility to step up to adulthood is the obvious one that adulthood can never be something with which you are endowed by someone else. Adulthood, by definition, is something we each as individuals achieve, or it is not really adulthood. Adulthood, in the church as in life, must be claimed. The difference is that when someone achieves the kind of

---

37. Even simple practices such as the common practice of bishops writing Ad Clera is illustrative of practices that reinforce clericalism. Firstly there is the use of the Latinism, and then, in my experience of fifteen years as a diocesan bishop, there were few occasions where the content of my regular letter to the clergy could not be shared more widely. Eventually I changed the title and opened it up to parish council chairs and wardens, as well as school heads and other agency leaders, writing specifically to the clergy only on those rare occasions when that was warranted.

38. Wilson, *Clericalism*, 21.

maturity that we recognize as true adulthood, families and friends find reason to celebrate, whereas adulthood in the church seems to be deplored.[39]

Then, even when the place of the laity is outwardly or officially celebrated, clericalism can persist in a myriad of what Maclean calls low-profile ways. The high-profile level of culture can be addressed through the familiar mechanisms of consultation, conversation, revised mission, and value statements, but it is the low-profile stuff, as he points out, that will either block progress or open the door. Most leaders committed to change will have had a "land mine" experience of low-profile culture, when some seemingly innocuous change or initiative erupts into a major organizational explosion. That which was innocuous and even taken for granted, when disturbed, reveals itself, often to everyone's surprise, as carrying a load of cultural dynamite. The encouraging converse of this negative is that careful attention and considered changes at the low-profile level can be powerful enablers of more extensive high-profile cultural change.[40] All this requires time.

Urgency and slowness

In the late 1990s and early 2000s, when an avalanche of sexual abuse revelations came into harsh light across a number of countries, the churches were accused quite rightly of responding too slowly. The survivors of abuse should have been responded to with greater urgency. Enhanced safeguarding procedures needed to be put in place quickly, screening systems upgraded, and safer ministry education programs put in place. This was the programmatic and structural response and it needed appropriate haste.

The challenge of culture change put to the churches by the Australian royal commission is more like the pilgrimage to Santiago de Compostela. It will take the long legs of time and determination, the walking pace that

---

39. Lakeland, *Catholicism at the Crossroads*, 104–23.

40. Maclean, *Leadership and Cultural Webs in Organisations*, 50–55. Maclean makes the point that while "high-profile symbols have the merit and convenience of being within the immediate and tight control of the prominent and powerful, they do not represent the means through which they can manage, direct, control or even change a culture." The reason for this, he suggests, is that the "high-profile" is always received through the interpretive framework of the "low-profile" (54).

allows for healing and yet continues on with perseverance.[41] Without this longer journey, addressing cultural issues like clericalism, the structural and programmatic measures put in place by churches in response to child abuse risks a slow and inevitable erosion.

---

41. In his book *Seeking the Church*, Stephen Pickard devotes a chapter to "Slow Church Coming," where he explores these themes: "'Jesus slow' indicates a particular kind of pace that enables healing and transformation. It is embedded in his walking on the land in the company of others." Pickard, *Seeking the Church*, 222.

Chapter 7

MOSES, MANAGEMENT, BISHOPS, BUDGETS, AND BUSYNESS

ORGANIZATIONS ARE AT THEIR most wholesome and best when leadership, structure, and culture complement and support each other. In many organizations, including the church, this sort of harmony can often be more assumed than actual, because as contexts and circumstances change, these important elements can easily move into discordant relationships. Leadership, organizational structures, and culture can find themselves disengaged from each other, or in conflict, so that forward progress grinds to a halt. If Moses had employed an organizational consultant, these things might have been explained to him early into the exodus journey, with the assistance of an environmental scan, SWOT analysis, and theoretical matrix. In the absence of such a specialist consultant, Moses had a canny father-in-law.

> The next day Moses sat as judge for the people, while the people stood around him from morning until evening. When Moses' father-in-law saw all that he was doing for the people, he said, "What is this that you are doing for the people? Why do you sit alone, while all the people stand around you from morning until evening?" Moses said to his father-in-law, "Because the people come to me to inquire of God. When they have a dispute, they come to me and I decide between one person and another, and I make known to them the statutes and instructions of God." Moses' father-in-law said to him, "What you are doing is not good. You will surely wear yourself out, both you and these people with you. For the task is too heavy for you; you cannot do it alone. Now

listen to me. I will give you counsel, and God be with you! You should represent the people before God, and you should bring their cases before God; teach them the statutes and instructions and make known to them the way they are to go and the things they are to do. You should also look for able men among all the people, men who fear God, are trustworthy, and hate dishonest gain; set such men over them as officers over thousands, hundreds, fifties, and tens. Let them sit as judges for the people at all times; let them bring every important case to you, but decide every minor case themselves. So it will be easier for you, and they will bear the burden with you. If you do this, and God so commands you, then you will be able to endure, and all these people will go to their home in peace." (Exod 18:13–27)

Moses began as the visionary leader of what Henry Mintzberg might have called an "autocracy" or "simple structure."[1] In Charles Handy's terminology, Moses is the "Zeus" leader, typical of a new organization where the founder is the only power, or the hands-on leader of an older organization in crisis.[2] When it comes to confronting pharaohs, calling down plagues, avoiding pursuit, and persuading a motley mob of beaten-down slaves to take the risk of freedom, this is the type of leadership structure you will probably want. Ideal as it was for an exodus from crisis, however, this organizational structure was never going to work for the long grind in the desert during the next part of the journey. Moses soon found himself exhausted by the demands of holding things together and the people started finding the bread of former times strangely attractive, as they tend to do when the organization they belong to enters arid and adverse places (Exod 16:3).

Moses listened to the advice of Jethro. He established structures of delegation with high levels of community ownership and autonomy, so that the people could "go to their homes satisfied" (18:23). These structural changes had an immediate cultural payoff, evidenced in the changed attitudes of the community; people began to feel at home. But deeper and more enduring changes were to follow. The rest of Exodus, more than half of the book, is devoted to a painstakingly detailed establishment of community

1. For a useful summary of organizational typologies, see McCann, *Church and Organization*, 50–53.

2. Handy, *Gods of Management*, 20–23. Zeus was the king of the Greek Gods who reigned on Mount Olympus by thunderbolts (when crossed) or showers of gold (when seducing). "He was feared, respected and occasionally loved. Zeus represented the patriarchal tradition, irrational, but often benevolent power, impulsiveness and charisma. Found in start-up situations of all sorts, and on the bridge of many a ship" (14).

law, symbols of identity, and rites of meaning. From this deep deposit of culture, Israel drew identity and direction as it entered the promised land, and still does today, as recalled in Passover remembrance:

> This is the bread of affliction,
> that our fathers ate in the land of Egypt.
> Whoever is hungry, let him come and eat;
> whoever is in need, let him come ...[3]

At critical times, this desert-shaped deposit of identity would be revisited and even reframed. When it came time for Israel to return from Babylon, that return was understood as a "new exodus," with the depth of cultural and theological content received into a new context and national structures. For those who remained in the diaspora, it remained a symbol of hope and unity: "Next year in Jerusalem." Jesus drew on this deposit to interpret his own death and resurrection as an "exodus," then reframed the Passover story in the Last Supper, making it a constitutive sign for the renewed community of his followers (Luke 9:31; 22:15).[4] Throughout the story of the people of God, there is this dynamic of the reconfiguring of social structures and leadership mixed with the reinterpretation of underlying culture and memory. This is the faithful interplay of a living tradition and vocation.

The dynamic today

Even in a time of rapid change, it sometimes takes a particular moment of crisis to highlight the accumulated effects of that ongoing change. For many churches, the scandal of child abuse has provided just such a moment of seeing how the increments of change had left the church out of step with the world around it and responding in ways that were contrary to its own foundational message.

In sections of its final report dealing with the Anglican and Roman Catholic churches in Australia, the royal commission was particularly scathing about how bishops contributed to the tragedy of abuse in terms of those critical categories that we referred to above—in their own leadership,

---

3. One of the prayers from a Passover Seder.

4. Often translated "departure," the word here is ἔξοδον (*exodov*—Luke 9:31), which gains significance from the company in which it is used (Moses and Elijah) and also from the subsequent words of Jesus: "I have earnestly desired to eat this Passover with you ..." (Luke 22:15).

within structures of governance, and in their responsibility for the culture of the dioceses they served.

Bishops assumed, or were put in the position of assuming, responsibility for matters in which they had insufficient expertise, underdeveloped and variable processes at their disposal, few structures of accountability or supervision, and around which they often had conflicts of interest. All these factors resulted in outcomes that were at times catastrophic, a "national tragedy."[5] It took a crisis to expose what had been developing for decades: a growing discord between the structures, leadership, and vocational culture of the church and its missional context.

Fifty years ago in Australia, and in many similar countries throughout the world, most of the functions necessary in an Anglican diocese could be held together at that diocesan level: pastoral care, social services, governance and administration. The world has changed dramatically. I spent four years as a diocesan bishop in a smaller country diocese and then eleven years as the bishop of a state capital diocese and archbishop in one of the Australian church's internal provinces. When I went as bishop to the Anglican Diocese of Adelaide in 2005, it was following a crisis as a result of multiple sexual abuse revelations and the forced early retirement of the previous archbishop, after expressions of no confidence by the Diocesan Council and Professional Standards Committee.

Working with others within the diocese to develop better systems to respond to the survivors of abuse, establishing "safer ministry" protocols and education, as well as fulfilling a mandated role in several clergy disciplinary processes, was almost all-absorbing. Funding responses to survivors required a painful review of diocesan staffing. In one very demanding time, I remember that the amount spent on legal advice and fees in one year was around the total budget of the smaller country diocese from which I had come. In the midst of this, and like most of my contemporaries in medium to larger dioceses, I found that I had an immediate governance relationship with a dozen or so other entities, including being a director on several boards, as well as membership of another bundle of committees. Midway through my time in Adelaide, the church's major social services organization, of which I was president and a director, AnglicareSA, employed about 1,500 people and had a budget of about $140 million (more than ten times the diocesan central budget). Some of these involvements needed, and in some instances required under law, close fiduciary attention. Yet at

---

5. Commonwealth of Australia, *Royal Commission Final Report*, 31–45.

this time, the community of the diocese itself was wounded and needed the pastoral closeness of its bishop.

What is remarkable about my experience is that there was actually nothing that remarkable about it; bishops in similar sized or larger dioceses in Australia, and throughout the churches of the Anglican Communion, will recognize the reality.

Alongside a few dioceses based in larger cities, more than half of the dioceses in Australia are small, widespread, and under-resourced. The constitution of the Anglican Church of Australia gives almost no executive capacity to national or even provincial structures, so the church has necessarily located much of its administrative, financial management, and compliance functions at the level of the individual diocese. With these smaller dioceses often struggling for viability and at the same time trying to manage the inevitable risks involved in operating institutions such as schools, aged care, and other agencies, the bishops of these dioceses often find themselves absorbed in institutional governance and management, knowing that the failure of a major agency could pull the whole diocese down.[6] Where a bishop has a suitable aptitude or background, these involvements can represent a critically important and positive intervention. Where otherwise able bishops find themselves out of their depth in these areas of governance, compliance, and risk, then the results can be catastrophic. In recent decades, several regional dioceses in Australia have been brought to their knees through the collapse of one or more diocesan institutions. But even where a bishop is capable in areas of institutional governance and administration, there is a price to pay in episcopal energy and missional relationality.

Different approaches but similar results

Whereas the Anglican Church of Australia, for its own historic reasons, has had to locate most administration and compliance "down" at the level of the local bishop and diocese, the Church of England has moved in the opposite direction. With a long history of centralized administrative and financial management, the Church of England has taken more of its

---

6. Smaller dioceses in Australia can cover vast areas and face the additional cost of doing so. The small Diocese of Willochra, for instance, has less than two dozen parishes, but covers an area about four times that of the UK. One of the former bishops of Willochra used a light plane to get around his diocese.

ministerial oversight and planning "up" into its centralized structures. This was most clearly evidenced in the establishment of the Archbishops' Council in 1999, which among other things provided for greater archiepiscopal oversight of the disbursements from the Church Commission. One effect of this change has been that ministerial strategy became increasingly driven, through resource allocations, at the archiepiscopal level rather than from within the individual diocese. Martyn Percy argues that, as a result of this shift, the Church of England has come to be dominated by "multiple layers of executive management," operating at the cost of theological reflection and wisdom.

> The current English archbishops are now functioning much-like corporate chief executives within their respective provinces and nationally. The role of a diocesan bishop is thereby reduced in scope to that of an area manager, left with targets, aims, objectives and outcomes set by executive managers, and endorsed by "visionary" archbishops. The bishops, as area managers, are further controlled through tightly regulated training processes. In all this, the parish clergy are reduced to the status of local branch managers, thinly stretched in resourcing, but made to chase the (unreachable) targets set by the area managers (bishops). Incentives and rewards (i.e., preferment, additional resourcing, etc.) are offered to those who deliver.[7]

What is striking is that through the centralizing of administration with archiepiscopal oversight in the English Church, and the dispersing of administration and compliance into every small diocese of the Australian Church, there are actually similar outcomes in both: the essential relationality of diocesan mission and episcopal leadership is seriously compromised. In both instances, episcopal ministry is captured by corporate and administrative functions. Pickard goes as far as to suggest that the environment in which most bishops now operate makes it nearly impossible for them to fulfill the vows of consecration:

> Under what kinds of conditions is it possible for bishops to fulfil their promise at consecration . . . Why is such a question on the agenda? Consulting a bishop's daily, weekly, monthly and yearly diary might offer a clue. This would tell the story of remarkable busyness, crowded days, few spare moments, rapid and constant travel between engagements, little space, time and peace for

---

7. Percy, "Emergent Archiepiscopal Leadership within the Anglican Communion."

critical reflection, let alone writing, and immersion in a host of ecclesiastical and secular appointments.

Who can undertake episcopal office in our present environment?[8]

Such analysis and critique is not intended to suggest that the church should be reluctant to avail itself of the best of administrative or structural models from the world around it. Quite to the contrary. The church has a responsibility of stewardship under God to the assets and resources committed to its care; and in terms of human resources, there is little doubt that there are elements of contemporary organizational models that are much more equitable and empowering than some of those with which the church continues to lumber on. There is every reason, then, why the church ought to be open to learning from the world around it. Percy's point is that in doing so, it should always be informed by deep, dense, and diverse reflection on its being and vocation. Bring in the external consultants? By all means, but first of all struggle with the ecclesiological questions, so that in any shift of structures, the fundamental mission of the local church is enabled and its leaders are "placed" to offer the relational oversight that is at the heart of their vocation.

Putting leaders in their place

In 1997, Stephen Pickard and I co-authored an article, "'Re-Placing' Bishops: An Ecumenical and Trinitarian Approach to Episcopacy."[9] The article was not suggesting that bishops be *replaced*, but that the church needed to explore ways to ensure that bishops and dioceses were *differently and better placed* to offer the key elements of episcopal ministry in a rapidly changing and complex context. What we proposed was the reconfiguring of dioceses around a more "natural" and "relational" episcopate.

> The focus here would not be territorial space nor cultural group but "place," identified in terms of the quality of social interactions and the potential for enriched communal life in society. This at least is what a contemporary trinitarian approach would seem to require with its strong emphasis upon the social dynamic of the gospel of a God whose own being is not solitary but a communion of persons. Yet in this proposal the natural features of the

---

8. Pickard, *Theological Foundations for Collaborative Ministry*, 171–72.
9. Pickard and Driver, "'Re-Placing' Bishops."

environment and geography, the natural reach and mobility of the inhabitants and their sense of the place they occupy would be some of the criteria important in recognizing and designating a natural place within which episcopal ministry could be exercised in its personal, pastoral and teaching dimensions.[10]

Politely received at the time, the basic argument of that article seems even more relevant today; in traditional churches with the episcopal polity and diocesan structures that history has provided, the fundamental ministerial structures of the church are either too large for relational mission, or too small for effective administration and the management of risk and compliance.

As the social scientists remind us, when it comes to organizations, size does matter. In a smaller grouping, influence can be personal and exercised in direct relationships, whereas in larger entities some form of legitimized power apparatus will be required, with the workings of power inevitably becoming remote, more hierarchical and inaccessible.[11] While there is no organizational size that is optimal in every instance, the ecclesiological challenge is to identify the structures and "placing" of leaders that best fits the church's being, mission, and contextual reality. These organizational arrangements can change from time to time and they have done so over the years. Pickard, Alan Brent, and more recently, Luke Hopkins are among Australian scholars who have looked at the development of episcopal ministry and the structures of the local church as they might inform contemporary Anglicanism.[12]

The model of episcopacy that emerged within the Roman Empire during the third century has often been called the Cyprianic model, not because Cyprian (200–258) invented this model, but because he was among those who gave it clear articulation.[13] In the Cyprianic model, the ministerial function of the bishop in community with the people of God began to be blended with a jurisdictional and geographic character similar to that of

---

10. Pickard and Driver, "'Re-Placing' Bishops," 27.

11. Luhmann, *Trust and Power*, 123. See also Weber, *Economy and Society*, 33–38, 212–15, 25–26.

12. Pickard, *Theological Foundations for Collaborative Ministry*, 177–82; Brent, *Cultural Episcopacy and Ecumenism*; Hopkins, "Cyprian of Carthage and the Australian Anglican Episcopate."

13. Hopkins, "Cyprian of Carthage and the Australian Anglican Episcopate," 26. "Cyprian's theology emerges not to create a new system of ecclesial governance but to reflect theologically on the patterns that were already widespread."

local government in the Roman Empire. This trend was accentuated under Constantine.[14] For Anglicans, then, it was further reinforced by centuries of establishment in England, with bishops appointed by the crown taking a place in secular government and accruing the trappings of privilege. It was then spread by the British Empire and colonial expansion around the globe.

There is little doubt that the Cyprianic way of being the local church had powerful cultural resonance through to more recent times. Until the latter part of the twentieth century, geography and jurisdiction were among the most prominent components of human identity and relationality. People lived and worked in local areas and identified with the social structures of that area. The local football team consisted of players from that city, county, shire, or state, and the player trade of modern times would have been considered a perplexing betrayal. With the nature of human relationality shifting, and continuing to shift in the digital age, church structures influenced by the semi-jurisdictional Cyprianic model, but without the cultural connections they once enjoyed, can struggle to resonate with the world around them.[15]

There are other models in the deposit of tradition. For all its influence, the Cyprianic model of bishop and diocese was preceded by an earlier form described in Irenaeus (130–202) which emphasized the bishop in the local church as authoritative teacher of the apostolic faith.[16] Earlier still, in

14. Gunton, "Church on Earth," 69. Gunton accepts the proposition that Cyprian's ideal of the church is derived in large measure by analogy with a political empire, "an aristocratically governed state with an ideal head." As we have noted, under Constantine, bishops could even have a judicial role that could extend beyond the Church into the wider community. For a helpful summary, see Burkhard, *Apostolicity Then and Now*, 216–17.

15. This is not to discount place entirely as a marker of community. Parts of Australia still strongly maintain identity through location, with church structures reflecting this reality. Tasmanians still tend to consider the Australian mainland to be an island off Tasmania; and try telling a Scot that there is little distinguish him from the sassenachs in London! However, humans born in the twenty-first century are born into locations that are digitally determined as much as geographically so. Their sense of place will be shaped as much by digital reach as neighborhood.

16. Sullivan, *From Apostles to Bishops*, 146. "The key idea for Irenaeus is that the apostles entrusted the safe-guarding and transmission of their message to those to whom they entrusted the care of the churches. The apostles handed on their own teaching office to those whom they left as successors [*quos et successors relinquebant, suum ipsorum locum magisterii tradentes*]." Here Irenaeus uses the term "bishops" of those appointed by the apostles with this teaching office. Writing as a bishop himself, Irenaeus was no doubt aware of the many pastoral duties incumbent upon bishops, but here he focuses on their role as transmitters of the teaching of the apostles.

Ignatius of Antioch (108–130), we find the bishop as very much the leaders of local churches supported by presbyters.[17] These models of episcopacy still prevail in the Orthodox Churches.

Various sizes might be proposed for a more relational episcopate, but there is little doubt that considerable downsizing would be required in major urban dioceses of 300–400 parishes. Former Anglican Church of Australia general secretary, Bruce Kaye, suggested that around thirty-five parishes with associated agencies as a number that would enable "genuine episcopacy."[18] That number is probably close to the bare minimum for staffing flexibility, but a size much beyond fifty to fifty-five parishes would make it difficult for a bishop to truly "know and be known" by the people of God, joining the clergy and laity in worship, prayer, and sacrament, and taking a personal interest in those training for ministry.[19] While there is undoubtedly a place for assisting bishops, particularly in providing oversight in specific or culturally distinctive situations, the presumption should be that when a diocese is too big for an effective and relational episcopate, then the default ought to be to look at reconfiguring the diocese.

The necessary corollary of reconfiguring in this way would be that some of the jurisdictional and administrative functions that have been located in the diocese as part of the Cyprianic legacy would also need to be "placed" differently, possibly in larger aggregations or entities.[20] Not only would this add to the missional freedom of the bishop and diocese, it would offer the possibility of greater efficiency and effectiveness in areas of increasing complexity and risk. Key to such arrangements working effectively would be accountability arrangements that ensured that the local diocese, bishop, and people in community retained the freedom to shape their mission together under God.

17. Sullivan, *From Apostles to Bishops*, 104–10.

18. Kaye, *Reinventing Anglicanism*, 259.

19. The Ordination of Bishops in *A Prayer Book for Australia*, 802. One of the other characteristics of the modern diocese is the number of office-holders that stand between a bishop and the need to "know and be known": archdeacons, canons, area deans, the list goes on.

20. There is a risk in this. The risk is that agencies can drift away from their ecclesial origins and vocation. Managing the relationship between dioceses and agencies, particularly larger agencies that receive government funding, can be a challenge. This is heightened when an agency is incorporated and then subject to corporate and charitable laws which, in Australia at least, can limit the influence the church can have in terms of policy and governance. Various approaches have been taken but there does not seem to be one prevailing model.

In some ways this emphasis on the relational and locally contextual is countercultural. The trend is towards globalization, whether in manufacturing, entertainment, or the fast food offered under golden arches. The ecclesiastical equivalent can be found in the international "network" churches such as the global Hillsong network that started as a suburban Pentecostal congregation in Sydney.[21] With congregations now in thirty countries, Hillsong is governed by a "global pastor" and board that determines and can terminate all appointments, ensure compliance to the Hillsong way of operating, and can veto most local decisions on a recommendation of the global pastor supported by the board.[22] It is a global franchise with all the quality control and appeal of a global franchise. For all that appeal and success, however, Hillsong represents a culturally colonizing way of being church, something that Anglicans should be able to recognize in their own history, but which stands in contradiction of the deeper ecclesiological principles of immersive and contextual mission.

God's global ambitions [*God so loved the world*] are always expressed in astounding particularity [*that he gave his only Son*] (John 3:16). This is the character of the *missio Dei*, in which the eternal and all-embracing is encountered in the skin and flesh, location and time, of one Jesus of Nazareth, and is carried forward in universal scope with the same particularity of cultural context and encounter.

In October 2021, Melbourne received the dubious honor of being the most locked down city on Earth.[23] In well-resourced and digitally connected suburbs, in a country with amongst the highest internet usage per person in the world, the constant complaint was that people simply ached to see each other face-to-face.[24] COVID-19 provided the worst kind of reminder that the actual presence of another, flesh and blood and the intimacies of small things shared, is an irreplaceable gift. At the heart of mission and of the

---

21. There have been, of course, "networks" of church plants established across Anglican dioceses in Australia and other countries. They have many of the same organizational traits as Hillsong even when they have their own style of worship or distinctive doctrines; strong central control as well as doctrinal and cultural uniformity.

22. Hillsong's "Global Governing Principles" are published online at https://hillsong.com/policies/global-governing-principles/.

23. On October 8, 2021, Melbourne overtook Buenos Aries as the most locked down city, with 246 days of COVID-19 lockdown.

24. One source lists at least occasional internet usage in Australia as 94 percent of the population—higher, for instance, than the UK (91 percent) and the US (90 percent). https://www.pewresearch.org/fact-tank/2020/04/02/8-charts-on-internet-use-around-the-world-as-countries-grapple-with-covid-19/.

church's being is the God who took "flesh and lived among us" (John 1:14). There might be much to gain for the church from high-level structures of administration, financial management, and compliance; there is undoubtedly much to learn from the organization and professional presentation of the global church franchises, but at the level of mission and ministry, the church needs to be configured around the relationality of taking flesh and living among us. As Hopkins puts it, "Our structures should fit our theology, rather than our theology being reformatted to suit our structures."[25]

Bishops as stewards of culture

The word for bishop, *episkopos*, comes from secular usage in New Testament times to describe a person who had responsibility for keeping watch, overseeing, or even standing guard. Some of these linguistic associations have passed directly into the language of the ordinals; bishops are to share with their fellow presbyters the *oversight* of the churches. They are to *guard* the faith, unity, and discipline of Christ's church. They are to *watch over*, protect, and serve.[26]

Modern usage of the term "overseer," however, would seem to suggest that episcopacy is about providing line supervision: management and control from above, like a foreman over a team of workers. There are some occasions when being a bishop may involve direct organizational supervision, but a deeper theological sense of episcopacy might be accessed simply by turning the two components of the word around. Instead of "over-seeing," it becomes "seeing over"—allowing one's sight to rest on the whole.

> Then Moses went up from the plains of Moab to Mount Nebo, to the top of Pisgah, which is opposite Jericho, and the Lord showed him the whole land: Gilead as far as Dan, all Naphtali, the land of Ephraim and Manasseh, all the land of Judah as far as the Western Sea the Negeb, and the Plain—that is, the valley of Jericho, the city of palm trees—as far as Zoar. (Deut 34:1–5)

Mount Nebo, in what is now Jordan, provides a high point of about eight hundred meters, allowing a panoramic vision over parts of the Red Sea, the Jordan River, and even Jerusalem. This is territory Moses would

---

25. Hopkins, "Cyprian of Carthage and the Australian Anglican Episcopate," 181.

26. The Ordination of a Bishop in *A Prayer Book for Australia*, and in *Common Worship* (the Church of England).

never traverse himself. Others would do that. His was to be given a glimpse of the spread of its landscape and to lead the people of God to a place from which they could enter it for themselves. It is a powerful image for episcopal ministry. A bishop is called to discern the ecclesial landscape of the church in its wholeness and to encourage the people of God to share in that seeing and so to go ahead into the land of their belonging.

In this the bishop has a particular stewardship of ecclesial identity and culture. Formally, or at what Mclean calls the high-profile level, ecclesial identity is often expressed in the traditional language of holiness, catholicity, and apostolicity.[27] Attending to ecclesial identity at this more formal and structural level involves the teaching role of the bishop, and sometimes the exercise of "discipline with mercy." These are important parts of the ministry of a bishop. But attending to the character marks of the church only at the formal level can have oppressive and distorting results; oneness can become institutional conformity, holiness can tend towards exclusivity, catholicity can become focused on formal continuity with the past, and apostolicity can lean towards doctrinal policing.

It is in the informal and relational that deeper levels of ecclesial identity be addressed. As Mclean points out, identity lives persistently at the low-profile level, in the assumed and habitual, the underlying predispositions, the unconsciously accepted ways of interacting and reacting that make up organizational or institutional culture. Edgar Schein argues that what a leader pays attention to is a primary mechanism for embedding culture within an organization; more important than organizational design and structure, systems and procedures, and even the physical space. This is another form of "seeing over," that involves a light touch of giving attention to the particular in light of a vision of the whole. This is a giving of attention that fulfills the consecration vow to "know and be known." This is the sort of attentiveness and prayerful "discerning of spirits" can easily be surrendered to an overscheduled diary, back-to-back meetings, and executive functions.[28]

---

27. McLean, *Leadership and Cultural Webs in Organisations*, 50–55. For a helpful contemporary discussion of the marks of the church, see Pickard, *Seeking the Church*, 131–42.

28. Schein (*Organizational Culture and Leadership*, 230–32). The idea of encouraging cultural change by attentiveness—"over-seeing"—accords well language of the ordinal: "You are to watch over . . . and to be hospitable . . . You must, therefore, know and be known by them, and be a good example to all" (*A Prayer Book for Australia*, 802) Schein's notion of attentiveness seems to imply an attention-giving that frees and encourages, not

Re-placing bishops, re-placing management

Whether in the complexities of the English Church, the business and busyness of an urban diocese, or the challenges of the far-flung and under-resourced ministry in the Australian bush, when episcopal ministry and management dance too close together, the risk is that the latter colonizes the former. In a complex world, both need to be placed where they function most effectively. The relationality of episcopacy needs to be tuned to the social dynamics of human community. For management and administration to be effectively resourced, some elements may need to operate on a larger, aggregated scale. The Cyprianic or Constantinian model of episcopal ministry and geographic jurisdiction welded together may need to be reworked for a different time.

---

the constant attention that stifles and stymies. Within the present diocesan structures, as we have suggested, it is difficult to give space to this sort of careful, but relaxed, attentiveness. As a diocesan bishop, I tried to elicit frank advice from time to time from some trusted lay colleagues. One person had a particular saying he would send in my direction from time to time: "Get out of the bike shed!" Bishops need spaces to step back from the "nuts and bolts" in order to attend to the "seeing over" that enables them to discern the church in the often mundane and sometimes precarious landscape of a diocese. The clergy and the people of the diocese, needless to say, as much as they value the attention of the bishop from time to time *also* value the freedom to get on with things themselves.

Chapter 8

SEARCHING OUT THE CHURCH IN THE SHADOWS OF SHAME

Church searching for church

THE COVID-19 PANDEMIC HAS provided a sad and salutary reminder that there are times when the church has to search out new ways of being. Ordinarily, if visitors to a town asked where they could find a church, they might be pointed to a prominent building, or given a street location where they would find a distinctive structure with a sign out front advertising worship times. During extended lockdowns, church buildings throughout the world were closed. Congregations could not meet, so even the slightly more refined understanding that the church was not the building, but the people that met together inside the building, had its challenges. Churches were forced to experiment with creative ways of keeping people connected; live streamed services, interactive worship and meetings by Zoom, Facebook, chatgroups, socially distanced outdoor gatherings, and for those who were digitally disadvantaged, sermons, reflections, and prayers delivered to the letter box. Then, when physical gatherings were allowed to resume, often with restricted numbers and requirements for social distancing, another range of options had to be explored. Different ways of administering the sacraments had to be adopted and were surprisingly accepted. Even the entrenched Anglican habit of sitting in the same place each Sunday had to be surrendered to the necessities of social distancing.

After a year or so of this, a fellow worshipper said to me that she "just wished we could get back to church as normal." I sympathized with her. The disruptions and limitations were frustrating. I later reflected, though, that in all the changes, accommodations, adjustments, and struggles, we were, in some ways, experiencing church "more normal," not less. If the presumption is that "normal" church is a settled thing to be repeated with only slight and minor variations week by week, then what we have experienced recently is certainly far from "normal." If, on the other hand, church is understood as by nature "not there yet," incomplete and contingent, called to constant exploration of ways to give social expression to the gospel of Christ, then the disruptions of the COVID-19 pandemic brought not just a "new normal," but an ecclesial "very much normal."[1]

The task of this book has been to explore some of the cultural and theological influences that may have predisposed church institutions and agencies to the possibility of abuse, defensive responses, and cover-up. One contributing factor, I have suggested, is the tendency for the church to forget that being "not there yet" is the ecclesial normal and therefore to put an idealizing halo over the "already" of its earthly life and structures. All human institutions tend to reify their own life and structures, but in the church, that tendency can easily be theologized into a sense of divine endorsement for things as they are, contributing to a culture of being beyond reproach, in which a lack of accountability is normalized and the abused feel too intimidated to have their voice heard.

The more authentic church is one that embraces fully the reality of "church searching for church," that knows it is still searching to find itself in fuller expression. To search is to recognize that there is more to be found and also to acknowledge that something important may be lost. Strange as it may sound, the church is most truly itself when it knows it must keep on searching out its true self; that is, when it recognizes its realities and neither idealizes them nor accepts them as inevitable.

For the church to speak more in the language of searching and journey, and less in the pronouncements of certainties delivered, is not somehow to compromise its witness to Christ as the one "in whom all the fulness of God was pleased to dwell" (Col 1:19). Rather it is to acknowledge, with the apostle Paul, that its apprehension of that fullness is at best partial, it

---

1. Once again, I am picking up a popular slogan that was also the title of a 2005 American family comedy film directed by Brian Levant. A book by the same title was published in Australia in 2004, with Alison Lester being the author.

is still seeing in a "mirror dimly," still awaiting the eschatological "then" of knowing and being fully known (1 Cor 13:12–13). Even to acknowledge that darkness and distortion can be found in the church, as in the world, does not take us beyond the biblical witness. We have noted already that the New Testament language about bondage to the "powers" and "elemental spirits" is actually applied as much to life within the church as to the world around it. The church "disarms" the worldly powers by firstly naming them within its own life.

Always frail, always subject to the fluctuations and infirmities of the human will and at risk of wandering from its way, "the whole church is the church of the penitent, the church of those who are perishing."[2] An indication that the church has begun a deeper cultural journey following the tragedy of abuse will be the careful and more honest use of the language of the fellow traveler. This should especially be so in the language of prayer and worship.

Even where churches have responded to failure by addressing structures and process, the previous culture can linger pervasively on, expressed at the low-profile level of symbol and habit, insider language and affectations—even in liturgical rites and how they are used. Beyond the language of safeguarding and the vocabulary of process, it is the language and gestures that the church uses when it celebrates and prays that speak most powerfully of what it is and what it is called to be. While the 1662 Book of Common Prayer might be characterized as having a tone primarily of reverential approach, the great majority of rites that emerged from the movement for liturgical renewal in the last half of the twentieth century gave much more place to celebrating salvation history, what God has done for and among the people of God. This shift had sound theological, historical, and liturgical foundations, but in a world characterized by postmodern cynicism about institutions, and within churches shamed by widespread revelations of abuse, some of the texts that undoubtedly seemed appropriate even two or three decades ago can seem a little too unqualified and jarring today.[3] The Eucharistic Thanksgiving for Easter Day in *A Prayer Book for Australia* provides an example. Of course it is true, theologically, to say:

2. Ephrem the Syrian, quoted in Vladimir Lossky, *Mystical Theology of the Eastern Church*, 180.

3. In the context of trauma, Shelly Rambo (*Spirit and Trauma*, 22–25) makes an interesting distinction between "witness" and "proclamation." In the place of trauma and shame, the notion of bearing witness seems more congruent than that of proclamation, at least in the unqualified sense in which proclamation might have a greater implication

> By his victory over death
> the reign of sin is ended
> a new day has dawned,
> a broken world is restored,
> and we are made whole once more.[4]

All these affirmations are already true in Christ. They are the gifts of Easter. But the church that is privileged to say these things is also the church that has seen numbers of its leaders abuse thousands of minors throughout the world and has, in some places, been complicit or negligent, allowing criminal cover-up and further suffering. The disciples to whom this joyful Easter proclamation is committed are also those who (then and now) have run away, resorted to denials, and stood at a distance while an innocent suffered (Matt 26:56, 69–75; 27:55). As part of a deeper response to what it has had to face in the crisis over abuse, it may be time, once again, for the church to bring some new language to fill out its vocabulary of prayer with more of the humility of "not there yet."

> In the darkness of our denial, you looked upon us in love,
> in the garden of our grief you call us by name.
> When we fled from suffering,
> you walked alongside us on the way.[5]

Owning the shadows

Shadows are the places where light and darkness mingle in the ambiguity of both and neither. Shadows are made up of the grey tones of the less-than-absolute, where shape is discerned only as time is taken for sight to adjust and the shades of nuance to emerge. In this book, I have traced some theological threads of institutionality and power within the people of God and suggested that when the church loses a sense of its own shadow side, the possibility of abuse is increased. One of the ways this happens, I proposed, is through the theological idealization of the institutional. Forgetting that all the organizational structures among God's people come from the necessities and convenience of adapting from the world around them ("appoint

---

of certainty and even superiority.

4. *Prayer Book for Australia*, 154.

5. Some ponderings from the Easter narrative that might be part of a eucharistic thanksgiving prayer.

for us a king . . . like other nations," 1 Sam 8:6–7) ecclesial structures can be divinized and the instruments of check and critique silenced. When this happens in Catholic expression, belonging becomes institutional compliance and institutional protection. In evangelical circles it becomes a matter of formulaic agreement. The prophets are stoned or forced out into the desert, if not literally anymore, at least in terms of influence and opportunity.

An equally worrying alternative to this is an ecclesiology based on retreat from what is regarded as worldly contamination. Historic expressions range from the Essenes in Palestine, the early rigorist movement in the early church, extreme monasticism, Puritanism, through to various apocalyptic movements in more recent times. Within the whole, they might be part of a necessary balancing, but when they are embraced as the only way, they too can become exclusivist and tyrannical.

Only an ecclesiology that gives full account of the historical "is" as much as the vocational "ought" can be offered after the shame of institutional failure. Part of the real church is its shadow side. Only an abstract and idealized ecclesiology can overlook that darker side of the church that always accompanies its historical form.

> Jerusalem, Jerusalem, the city that kills the prophets and stones those who are sent to it! How often have I desired to gather your children together as a hen gathers her brood under her wings, and you were not willing! (Luke 13:34)

As necessary as they are, all institutions will lean towards the coercive and, as the sociologists remind us, this includes the institutions of religion. All institutions dispose power and inevitably do so in some degree of disproportionality and this, too, is inevitably the case in religious institutions. All institutions have a default towards self-protection, even when it is unacknowledged or disguised by ideology. These are some of the institutional grey spaces that the historical church inhabits. When they are not acknowledged and taken up into the church's self-naming that we call ecclesiology, the risk is that they become daemonic and legion.

An ecclesiology that includes a mature perspective on institutionality and power within the people of God will be expressed in an affirmed space for conflict, critique, and sustained disagreement.[6] This provides a response

---

6. Despite King David being something of a rogue, it was in his openness to hear the sharpness of the prophet Nathan, that his reign was elevated as an example for those that followed.

to the culture of compliance that has been identified as leading to the possibility of abuse and cover-up.

Within the church, the development of the Cyprianic model of episcopacy as outlined above, followed by the assertion of an imperial form of papal supremacy in the Western church, there was little place for loyal opposition let alone sustained criticism. This was one of the factors that prompted the conciliar movement and which was taken up by the Reformers in their plea for the restoration of ecumenical councils.[7] As the principle of conciliarity was taken up in the English Reformation, the Parliament and Convocation were constituted as balancing authorities, lay and clerical, working through the principle of consent.[8] With convocation prorogued, these principles of conciliarity and consent were taken up in the development of modern synods, so that in most synods throughout the Anglican Communion measures may be considered by the each of three houses, that of the bishop, the clergy, and the laity, with the consent of each required.[9] This Anglican method of consensual working does offer a voice of critique or concern in governance of the churches, but synods are not entirely without their own dynamics of coercion. The swell of a movement through the houses of a diocesan synod takes courage to resist and the hesitant or uncertain member can feel pressured to go with the prevailing momentum. What amounts to a virtual veto in the House of Bishops in many Anglican dioceses, sits there in the background and can have its own persuasive effect.[10]

Without needing fundamental changes to their existing structure, synods could be used much more effectively as instruments of accountability and review. With greater intentionality, and perhaps some external assistance in developing criteria, the very visibility of synod processes can be used as an instrument of much greater accountability, even for agencies not

---

7. Avis, *Beyond the Reformation?*, 22–24, 134–49.

8. Avis (*Beyond the Reformation?*, 139) makes the point that Jewel was "insistent that the English Reformation had not been conducted without councils, assemblies, conferences of learned men, etc., particularly in Parliament and Convocation."

9. There is some variation from province to province. In Aoteaoroa New Zealand, for instance, the church works through three governing strands, or tikanga, each having the equivalents of diocesan synods operating through the formal principle of consent, though in Te Pīhopatanga o Aotearoa and Tikanga Pasefika there is a strong cultural valuing of decision through consensus.

10. In Australia, and in other parts of the Anglican Communion, the House of Bishops at the diocesan level has only one member, the diocesan bishop. In other provinces the assistant and coadjutor bishops are part of the House of Bishops.

directly under synodical governance.[11] The sentiment that disagreement, critique, and conflict are somehow expressions of disloyalty in the "diocesan family" often prevails in the church, so affirmed spaces for critique and dissent may need to be actively provided, without compromising the necessity for hard decisions to be made and appropriate authority honored.[12] At an individual level, the processes of feedback and review can be imbedded as part of an accountability culture, but again, the caution of Pickard and Percy needs to be heard; as these processes are adopted often from the corporate world, they need to be adapted to have a genuinely ecclesial focus.

The shadows of shame

The shame of abuse casts long shadows. Without detracting from a primary focus on immediate survivors, an understanding of cultural change in the church following the revelations of abuse needs to take into account the secondary effects of trauma and shame. Just as trauma can psychologically paralyze and blind individuals, so secondary trauma can have similar effects on institutions. "The perplexing space of survival," Shelly Rambo calls it, where individuals and communities experience paralysis—the inability to see, the inability to move beyond.[13] We see it in John's story of Mary Magdalene (John 20:11–18):

> As she wept, she bent over to look into the tomb and she saw two angels in white, sitting there where the body of Jesus had been lying, one at the head and the other at the feet. They said to her, "Woman, why are you weeping?" She said to them, "They have taken away my Lord, and I do not know where they have laid him."

---

11. In 2005, the Diocese of Adelaide invited a prominent survivor of sexual abuse from within its own life to address the synod. Although this was just before my time in the diocese, I know that the effect was profound, shifting attitudes and awareness, and informing the ongoing development of a diocesan response. Reports to diocesan synod, in my experience, tend to be seen as opportunities for advertising, promotion, and affirmation—and by some synod members as the opportunity to slip out for coffee. With carefully developed criteria and explicit focus, these reports could be much more significant instruments of accountability.

12. Radner and Turner (*Fate of Communion*, 129) argue that it is a particular role of the episcopate to help hold open a "space in time" to allow the airing of differences, while at the same time maintaining unity.

13. Rambo, *Spirit and Trauma*, 96–110. See also Herman, *Trauma and Recovery*, 51–95.

> When she had said this, she turned around and saw Jesus standing there, but she did not know it was Jesus . . ."

The vision of hope eludes her downcast eyes. That is how it is with those in the grey light of trauma. They see only graveclothes. They are still caught in seeing only that which has died. They do not understand the strange figures speaking of life. They struggle to recognize the friendship of someone coming alongside as they try to walk down the road away from their pain. In the shadows of shame and trauma, the messengers of hope seem to be talking idle nonsense.

In terms of the biblical narrative, this is the Holy Saturday experience, but not to be understood in the linear and sequential way that days are often understood, or in which the church's liturgical celebrations move us quickly from Good Friday to Easter Day, with Holy Saturday being little more than a halftime break.

Here we are on Good Friday and we are confronted with unspeakable trauma and our own complicity and negligence, at least vicariously, tied up in it all. So much suffering; no one can bear it. He cries out: "It is finished" and it comes to an end. Yet for the disciples, it is an end that does not feel like an end. They are shattered. Their trauma continues. It intensifies in emptiness. It takes over and drains them of energy and vision.

"But wait!" we want to say. "It will all be better soon!" And we race on to Easter Day and hymns of victory. Death is vanquished. Alleluia! Let's roll out the child protection programs and then get on with the strategic planning! But the Holy Saturday journey of deep cultural change takes as long as it takes, and it requires that as a church, we linger in the greyness long enough to hear the true calling of our name once more.

AN AFTERWORD
The Emmaus Road to Recognition

ONE OF THE MOST powerful moments for me, as I struggled with the effects of abuse in a hurt and grieving diocese, came surprisingly at a gathering of bishops. It was, if anything *the* gathering of bishops—the Lambeth Conference of 2008—and it was not the wounds within my diocese that came to the fore, but the wounds within myself.

During the conference, a part-day was set aside for the spouses of bishops to lead the gathering. I have long legs, so to give myself some leg-stretching space, I chose to sit in the front row-center. Another Australian bishop sat with me. It was in a massive marquee. There were about 1,700 people in all—bishops, spouses, and others—packed in for the session, which was called "Equal in God's Sight: When Power is Abused."

A small theater group presented a play based around a series of biblical figures: the woman taken in adultery, the woman with the flow of blood, the prodigal daughter (not son—a creative innovation). It captured in drama the grief of people being abused in the name of God by people in power.

I am not sure whether it was the fact that I was half a world away from my own ministry context, or that in some way the drama through its very nature, infiltrated its way through my psychological protections, or whether (dare I say it?) it was just a moment of God's Spirit.[1] But I found myself weeping. Not just shedding a tear, but weeping with a deep, from-the-gut grief. I was glad of my friend who simply laid a hand on my shoulder.

When that moment in Canterbury occurred, I had been archbishop of Adelaide for about two and a half years. I had come to the diocese after

---

1. Van der Kolk, *Body Keeps the Score*, 334–37. Van der Kolk actually makes the point that theater is a powerful tool for the treatment of trauma, as are other arts where the senses are engaged.

it had been the subject of national focus in regard to revelations of widespread historic abuse; an alleged perpetrator had committed suicide, the report of a board of inquiry had been tabled in state parliament, and the archbishop's handling of the matter had resulted in a vote of no confidence by the diocesan council, then his resignation. Those first two years had been spent trying to develop a response to the survivors of abuse, spending time hearing their stories (when that was what they wanted), and offering an apology personally. Significant time had to be spent on improving the child protection processes of the diocese and also developing a strategy to finance redress payments, with painful results in terms of staffing and morale.

It took a biblical drama under canvas in Canterbury to release the stress and grief of it all. I knew the drama was just the trigger. And I knew that when I returned home, I needed to get some help to deal with what was happening within and how that was affecting those who were close to me. On returning to Australia, I sought out a clinical professional to work with, and a journey towards some understanding and healing began. For nearly all the rest of my time in Adelaide I traveled interstate every few months to spend time with a health professional, a psychiatrist whose practice had a focus on dealing with abuse and trauma, including secondary trauma in both individuals and communities.[2]

As well as helping me come to grips with the depth of my emotional pain, she was insightful enough to determine that part of what would help me was some cognitive understanding of what was going on within and around me. We talked and she would give me the occasional reference to follow up on, or article to read. One of the things that I found particularly helpful was a better understanding of how ongoing exposure to trauma triggers the defensive mechanisms of fight and flight into hypersensitivity.[3] For me, "flight" took the form of a sort of personal withdrawal that

---

2. For a useful study into the effects of vicarious trauma, see Steed and Downing, "Vicarious Traumatisation."

3. Van der Kolk, *Body Keeps the Score*, 46–47, 82–83. Under normal conditions people react to a threat with a temporary increase in their stress hormones. The stress hormones of people who have experienced significant trauma, however, take much longer to return to their "baseline" and "spike quickly and disproportionately" in response to even mildly stressful stimuli. People get "stuck" in the modes of fight and flight, with often long-term effects on their neurochemical systems. As I understand it, this can occur in instances of both primary and secondary trauma. Van der Kolk actually speaks about three responses—fight, flight, and paralysis—the latter being the last resort, expressed in collapse and disengagement. See also Van der Kolk, "Black Hole of Trauma," 13–14.

could easily be experienced as aloofness or even rejection. As best I could, I curbed the "fight" impulse, the tendency to aggression or confrontation that comes with being affected by trauma. After all, I did not need a health professional to tell me that this was most likely an unproductive strategy for a bishop called to a grieving diocese! But curbing an impulse does not necessarily take it out by the roots and I am sure that people picked up tension or impatience in me from time to time in ways that were unhelpful.

I began to better understand what was happening inside me, and some of the places it was coming from. In particular, I came to see how plunging myself, without adequate self-care, into so much trauma and grief was actually triggering some of my own worst defaults and negatively affecting my relationships with those whom Jesus had called me to serve. Healing and ease slowly came. I had some years on medication; I found that humiliating, but understood the need. I began to make some simple changes as to how I managed my week, how I scheduled the number of difficult interviews in any day. I took my personal assistant into my confidence about these things so that she could help. Sometimes it was a matter of small and simple steps. I tried to make a ritual of a genuine lunch hour and to go home for it when I could, to walk in the garden, to say hello to the dog, and maybe even pull out a weed or two. In time, I shared much of this story with the diocesan council and they responded with real support.

In all this, there was some very real pain of discovery, but an unfathomable grace as well, including through some of the survivors of abuse. It was a journey of personal healing, but also one of better understanding as to how trauma affects whole communities. My initial frustration at what seemed to be low energy levels in the diocese, caution, and even cynicism, was changed as I came to understand more deeply how withdrawal and disengagement are an almost inevitable early response to a significant experience of trauma, even of a secondary nature. It was a road to Emmaus response. Faced with overwhelming trauma and grief, the understandable response of individuals and communities is to try to put it at all at some distance:

> Now on that same day two of them were going to a village called Emmaus, about seven miles from Jerusalem, and talking with each other about all these things that had happened. While they were talking and discussing, Jesus himself came near and went with them, but their eyes were kept from recognizing him. And he said to them, "What are you discussing with each other while you walk along?" They stood still, looking sad. Then one of them, whose

name was Cleopas, answered him, "Are you the only stranger in Jerusalem who does not know the things that have taken place there in these days?" He asked them, "What things?" They replied, "The things about Jesus of Nazareth, who was a prophet mighty in deed and word before God and all the people, and how our chief priests and leaders handed him over to be condemned to death and crucified him. But we had hoped that he was the one to redeem Israel."

As the story begins, we have two disciples on the road from Jerusalem to Emmaus. For Luke, as the scholars would suggest, the *from* of this journey is more important than the *to*. For Luke, Jerusalem is the city of weeping and the city of destiny (Luke 19:41–44). It is the place that Jesus travels *to* through most of Luke's first book, which we know as Luke's Gospel, and it is the place that the church travels *from* in his second book, the Acts of the Apostles. On the road to Emmaus, the disciples are hurrying away *from* the city which for them is only the city of grief. And as they travel, they remember; they recount "all these things that had happened." The scenes are being replayed, rerun, over and over again. They relive the horror and, like so many survivors of trauma, they are stuck in a pattern that cannot offer hope.

Seemingly out of nowhere, Jesus joins them, but there is no recognition because the only Jesus they can envisage is the one who is lost to them, except in their repeated recollections. But he journeys beside them, silently at first. After a time, he asks some question and they travel together for the rest of the way. When they reach Emmaus and their stranger-companion looks to be leaving to go his own way, they urge him to remain with them:

> "Stay with us, because it is almost evening and the day is now nearly over." So he went in to stay with them.

Jesus goes in with them and they partake of a simple travelers' meal. Jesus takes bread, blesses and breaks it, and in this simple oft-repeated action, their eyes are opened. Serene Jones comments:

> In this moment, we find the reality of grace breaking into their midst, not through an act of exclusionary compassion, but rather through a bodily gesture that is deeply embracing. This is no escapist meal of commodified junk food, a sharing of surface pleasures; it is a meal that nourishes and strengthens, and most importantly, it is a meal that opens their eyes. They see differently. The repetitive cycle is broken, and their imaginations are re-framed around

a shared table, not set to celebrate a vengeful patriotic victory, but a table of healing and fellowship.[4]

Because of the way trauma can affect our capacity to recognize and process, so often the most important moments of "seeing" come through a moment of lived experience.[5] They recognized Jesus when he broke the bread. The concrete, the visual, the tactile, can open the door to an exploration of pain and grace, just as that experience of drama touched me deeply at Lambeth and began a healing journey.[6]

There are no shortcuts on the road to Emmaus. That journey from Jerusalem cannot be measured simply by its seven miles. It unfolds of its own accord, at least if it is to culminate in a moment of recognition and returning. The journey that began for me in a poignant moment in Canterbury has continued through into this book and it is offered to encourage the church in the Emmaus journey of theological reflection and cultural change; from the dark shadows of shame to profound recognition and calling once more.

> They said to each other, "Were not our hearts burning within us while he was talking to us on the road, while he was opening the scriptures to us?"

The disciples immediately take to the road again. This time they are going back to what in Luke is always the city of destiny, Jerusalem the city of God. There, they join with others to become the church.

---

4. Jones, *Trauma and Grace*, 40.

5. Rambo, *Spirit and Trauma*, 17.

6. I was deeply impressed by the work of an artist friend in Brisbane who was involved in art therapy with service veterans. They met weekly to make pottery, to literally get their hands into the mud. The army did not quite understand, my friend suspected, but they were supportive. And the veterans—people who had served in places like Iraq and Afghanistan—valued their time together. My friend did not intrude—did not seek to address their pain directly—but she had a sense that something deep was happening.

BIBLIOGRAPHY

Anderson, Bernhard W. *The Living World of the Old Testament*. 4th ed. London: Longmans, 1988.
Anderson, Michael, and Miranda Jefferson. *Transforming Organizations: Engaging the 4cs for Powerful Organizational Learning and Change*. New York: Bloomsbury Business, 2019.
Anglican Church of Australia. *A Prayer Book for Australia; for use Together with the Book of Common Prayer (1662) and an Australian Prayer Book (1978)*. Alexandria, NSW: Broughton, 1995.
Anglican Church of Australia, Doctrine Commission. "Deposition from Holy Orders." https://anglican.org.au/wp-content/uploads/2019/11/1527-GS17-Report-Doctrine-Commission.pdf.
Anonymous. *An admonition to Parliament*. https://quod.lib.umich.edue/e/eebo/A00718. 0001.001?rgn=main;view=fulltext.
Arbuckle, Gerald A. *Abuse and Cover-Up: Refounding the Catholic Church in Trauma*. Maryknoll, NY: Orbis, 2019.
———. *Catholic Identity or Identities? Refounding Ministries in Chaotic Times*. Collegeville, MN: Liturgical, 2013.
———. *Change, Grief, and Renewal in the Church: A Spirituality for a New Era*. Westminster, MD: Christian Classics, 1991.
———. *Culture, Inculturation, and Theologians: A Postmodern Critique*. Collegeville, MN: Liturgical, 2010.
———. *Refounding the Church: Dissent for Leadership*. Maryknoll, NY: Orbis, 1993.
———. *Violence, Society, and the Church: A Cultural Approach*. Collegeville, MN: Liturgical, 2004.
Arndt, William, and F. Wilbur Gingrich. *A Greek-English Dictionary of the New Testament and Other Early Christian Literature*. 2nd ed. Chicago: University of Chicago Press, 1979.
Augustine. *City of God*. Lanham, MD: Start Publishing, 2012. https://search-ebscohost-com.divinity.idm.oclc.org/login.aspx?direct=true&db=nlebk&AN=669399&site=eds-live.
———. *The Trinity*. In *Augustine: Later Works*. Translated by John Burnaby. Library of Christian Classics Vol. 8. London: SCM, 1955.
Avis, Paul. *Anglicanism and the Christian Church: Theological Resources in Historical Perspective*. Minneapolis: Fortress, 1989.

———. *Authority, Leadership, and Conflict in the Church*. Philadelphia: Trinity Press International, 1992.

———. *Beyond the Reformation? Authority, Primacy and Unity in the Conciliar Tradition*. London: T & T Clark, 2006.

———. *Seeking the Truth of Change in the Church: Reception, Communion, and the Ordination of Women*. London: T & T Clark, 2004.

Beale, G. K. *The Book of Revelation: A Commentary on the Greek Text*. The New International Greek Testament Commentary. Grand Rapids: Eerdmans; Paternoster, 1999.

Benkert, Marianne, and Thomas P. Doyle. "Clericalism, Religious Duress and its Psychological Impact on Victims of Clergy Sexual Abuse." *Pastoral Psychology* 58.3 (Jun 2009), 223–38.

Berger, Peter L. *The Sacred Canopy: Elements of a Sociological Theory of Religion*. 1st ed. Garden City, NY: Doubleday, 1967.

Berger, Peter L., and Thomas Luckmann. *The Social Construction of Reality: A Treatise in the Sociology of Knowledge*. London: Penguin, 1967.

Berkhof, Hendrikus. *Christ and the Powers*. Translated by John H. Yoder. Scottdale, PA: Herald, 1962.

Black, Max. *The Social Theories of Talcott Parsons: A Critical Examination*. Englewood Cliffs, NJ: Prentice-Hall, 1961.

Borg, Marcus. *Jesus a New Vision: Spirit Culture and the Life of Discipleship*. San Francisco: Harper & Row, 1987.

Bouteneff, Peter C., and Alan D. Falconer. *Episkopé and Episcopacy and the Quest for Visible Unity: Two Consultations*. Geneva: WCC, 1999.

Brent, Allen. *Cultural Episcopacy and Ecumenism: Representative Ministry in Church History from the Age of Ignatius of Antioch to the Reformation, with Special Reference to Contemporary Ecumenism*. Leiden: E. J. Brill, 1992.

———. *Ignatius of Antioch: A Martyr Bishop and the Origin of Episcopacy*. London: Continuum, 2007.

Brett, Mark G. *Locations of God: Political Theology in the Hebrew Bible*. New York: Oxford University Press, 2019.

Bridges, William, and Susan Mitchell Bridges. *Managing Transitions: Making the Most of Change*. 4th ed. Boston: Da Capo Lifelong Books, 2016.

Brown, Peter. *The Rise of Western Christendom: Triumph and Diversity, AD 200–1000*. 2nd ed. Oxford: Blackwell, 2003.

Brueggemann, Walter. *Genesis*. Interpretation: A Bible Commentary for Teaching and Preaching. 1st ed. Louisville: Westminster John Knox, 2010.

Brunner, Emil. *The Misunderstanding of the Church*. London: Lutterworth, 1952.

Burkhard, John J. *Apostolicity Then and Now: An Ecumenical Church in a Postmodern World*. Collegeville, MN: Liturgical, 2004.

Caird, G. B. *Principalities and Powers: A Study in Pauline Theology*. The Chancellor's Lectures for 1954 at Queen's University. Oxford: Clarendon, 1956.

Carson, D. A. *Biblical Interpretation and the Church: Text and Context*. Exeter: Paternoster, 1984.

Chadwick, Henry. *The Church in Ancient Society: From Galilee to Gregory the Great*. Oxford: Oxford University Press, 2001.

———. *The Early Church*. Rev. ed. London: Penguin, 1993.

Chadwick, Owen. *The Spirit of the Oxford Movement: Tractarian Essays*. Cambridge: Cambridge University Press, 1990.
Chrétien, Jean-Louis. *The Call and the Response*. Perspectives in Continental Philosophy. 1st English language ed. New York: Fordham University Press, 2004.
Church of England, Archbishops' Review Group. *Resourcing Bishops: The Second Report of the Archbishops' Review Group on Bishops' Needs and Resources*. London: Church House, 2000.
Clark, Mary T., ed. *An Aquinas Reader*. With an introduction by Mary T. Clark. London: Hodder & Stoughton, 1974.
Cobble, James F. *The Church and the Powers: A Theology of Church Structure*. Peabody, MA: Hendrickson, 1988.
Coco, Angela. *Catholics, Conflicts and Choices: An Exploration of Power Relations in the Catholic Church*. Gender, Theology and Spirituality. Durham: Acumen, 2013.
Collins, John N. *Diakonia: Re-Interpreting the Ancient Sources*. Oxford: Oxford University Press, 1990.
Commonwealth of Australia. *Royal Commission into Institutional Responses to Child Sexual Abuse, Final Report*, Volume 16 Book 1. 2017. https://www.royalcommission.gov.au/child-abuse/final-report.
Conrad, Peter. *Modern Times, Modern Places*. 1st American ed. New York: Knopf, 1999.
Cranfield, C. E. B. *The Gospel According to Saint Mark: An Introduction and Commentary*. 1st ed., reprinted with revised additional supplementary notes. Cambridge: Cambridge University Press, 1979.
Crouse, Robert C. "Luther's 'Inward/Outward' Two Kingdoms." In *Two Kingdoms & Two Cities: Mapping Theological Traditions of Church, Culture, and Civil Order*, 4–8. Minneapolis: Fortress, 2017.
———. *Two Kingdoms & Two Cities: Mapping Theological Traditions of Church, Culture, and Civil Order*. Minneapolis: Fortress, 2017.
Curnow, Andrew and Stephen Hale, eds. *Facing the Future: Bishops Imagine a Different Church*. Melbourne: Acorn, 2009.
Douglas, Mary. *Natural Symbols: Explorations in Cosmology*. Routledge Classics. London: Routledge, 2003.
———. *Purity and Danger: An Analysis of Concepts of Pollution and Taboo*. Pelican Books. Harmondsworth: Penguin, 1970.
Driver, Jeffrey W. *A Polity of Persuasion: Gift and Grief of Anglicanism*. Eugene, OR: Cascade, 2014.
Dulles, Avery. *Models of the Church*. 2nd ed. Dublin: Gill and Macmillan, 1988.
Dunn, James D. G. *Jesus Remembered*. Grand Rapids: Eerdmans, 2003.
———. *A New Perspective on Jesus: What the Quest for the Historical Jesus Missed*. Grand Rapids: Baker Academic, 2005.
Durkheim, Emile. *The Elementary Forms of Religious Life*. Scotts Valley, CA: CreateSpace, 2014.
Esler, Philip Francis. *Community and Gospel in Luke-Acts: The Social and Political Motivations of Lucan Theology*. Monograph Series/Society for New Testament Studies. Cambridge: Cambridge University Press, 1987.
———. *The First Christians in Their Social Worlds: Social-Scientific Approaches to New Testament Interpretation*. London: Routledge, 1994.
Evans, G. R., and Martyn Percy. *Managing the Church?* Sheffield: Sheffield Academic, 2000.

Feldmeier, Reinhard. *Power, Service, Humility: A New Testament Ethic.* ProQuest Ebook Central: Baylor University Press, 2014. http://ebookcentral.proquest.com/lib/undiv/detail.action?docID=1637549.

Fleming, E. J. *Death of an Altar Boy: The Unsolved Murder of Danny Croteau and the Culture of Abuse in the Catholic Church.* Jefferson, NC: Exposit, 2018.

Foh, Susan. "What Is the Woman's Desire." *Westminster Theological Journal* 37 (1975) 376–83.

Forbes, Chris. "Paul's Principalities and Powers: Demythologizing Apocalyptic?" In *Journal for the Study of the New Testament* 23.82 (2001) 61–88. https://doi.org/10.1177%2F0142064X0102308203.

Frame, T. R. *Moral Injury: Unseen Wounds in an Age of Barbarism.* Sydney, NSW: New South Publishing, 2015.

Gaillardetz, Richard R. *Ecclesiology for a Global Church: A People Called and Sent.* Theology in Global Perspective. Maryknoll, NY: Orbis, 2008.

Gallagher, Michael Paul. *Clashing Symbols: An Introduction to Faith and Culture.* New York: Paulist, 1998.

Geertz, Clifford. *The Interpretation of Cultures: Selected Essays.* London: Hutchinson, 1975.

Giddens, Anthony. *The Constitution of Society: Outline of the Theory of Structuration.* Cambridge: Polity, 1984.

———. "'Power' in the Recent Writings of Talcott Parsons." *Sociology* 2.3 (September 1968) 257–72. https://doi.org/10.1177/003803856800200301.

Gill, Robin. *Theology and Sociology: A Reader.* New and enlarged ed. New York: Cassell, 1996.

Goldingay, John. *Genesis.* Baker Commentary on the Old Testament Pentateuch. Grand Rapids: Baker Academic, 2020.

Gore, Charles. *Orders and Unity.* London: John Murray, 1909.

Granfield, Patrick. "The Church as Societas Perfecta in the Schemata of Vatican I." In *Church History* 48.4 (1979) 431–46.

Greenwood, Robin. *Transforming Church: Liberating Structures for Ministry.* London: SPCK, 2002.

Greenwood, Royston. *The Sage Handbook of Organizational Institutionalism.* 2nd ed. Thousand Oaks, CA: SAGE, 2017.

Gunton, Colin. "The Church on Earth: The Roots of Community." In *On Being the Church: Essays on Christian Community*, edited by Colin Gunton and Daniel Hardy, 48–80. London: T & T Clark, 1989.

Gunton, Colin E., and Daniel W. Hardy, eds. *On Being the Church: Essays on the Christian Community.* London: T & T Clark, 1989.

Habel, Norman C. "Introducing Ecological Hermeneutics. In *Exploring Ecological Hermeneutics*, edited by Norman C. Habel and Peter L. Trudinger, 1–8. Atlanta: SBL, 2008.

Hall, Stuart George. *Doctrine and Practice in the Early Church.* 2nd North American ed. Eugene, OR: Cascade, 2011.

Handy, Charles B. *Gods of Management.* Oxford: Oxford University Press, 1995.

Hardy, Dan. *Finding the Church: The Dynamic Truth of Anglicanism.* London: SCM, 2001.

Harrington, Daniel J. *The Church According to the New Testament: What the Wisdom and Witness of Early Christianity Teach Us Today.* Franklin, WI: Sheed & Ward, 2001.

Harvey, Graham. *Religions in Focus: New Approaches to Tradition and Contemporary Practices*. Oakville, CT: Equinox, 2009.
Healy, Nicholas M. *Church, World, and the Christian Life: Practical-Prophetic Ecclesiology*. Cambridge Studies in Christian Doctrine. Cambridge: Cambridge University Press, 2000.
Heclo, Hugh. *On Thinking Institutionally*. On Politics. Oxford: Oxford University Press, 2008.
Hegstad, Harald. *The Real Church: An Ecclesiology of the Visible*. Church of Sweden Research Series. Eugene, OR: Pickwick, 2013.
Heine, Ronald E. "The Christology of Callistus." *The Journal of Theological Studies* 49.1 (1998) 56–91. https://www.jstor.org/stable/23968209?refreqid=excelsior%3A3fa8667b54b80cb30e79565b1612e81f.
Henn, William. "Apostolic Continuity of the Church and Apostolic Succession." *Louvain Studies* 21.2 (1996) 183–99. http://dx.doi.org/10.2143/ls.21.2.583432.
Herman, Judith Lewis. *Trauma and Recovery*. Rev. ed. New York: Basic, 1997.
Hippolytus. "Refutation of All Heresies." In *Writings from the Greco-Roman World*, edited by M. David Litwa, 655. Atlanta: SBL, 2016.
Hooker, Richard. *Of the Laws of Ecclesiastical Polity: A Critical Edition with Modern Spelling*. Edited by Arthur Stephen McGrade. Oxford: Oxford University Press, 2013.
———. *Of the Laws of Ecclesiastical Polity*. Edited by Paul G. Stanwood. Cambridge, MA: Belknap, 1981.
———. *Richard Hooker on Anglican Faith and Worship: Of the Laws of Ecclesiastical Polity, Book V: A Modern Edition*. Edited by Philip Bruce Secor. London: SPCK, 2003.
———. *Richard Hooker: Ecclesiastical Polity*. Edited by Arthur Pollard. London: Longmans, 1966.
———. *The Folger Library Edition of the Works of Richard Hooker (TFLE): Commentary, Books I–IV*. Introductions; Commentary. Edited by W. Speed Hill. John E. Booty, Georges Edelen, Lee W. Gibbs, William P. Haugaard, and Arthur Stephen McGrade, contributing editors; with the assistance of Egil Grislis. 6 vols. Vol. 6 Part 1. Binghamton, NY: Medieval & Renaissance Texts & Studies, 1993.
———. *The Folger Library Edition of the Works of Richard Hooker (TFLE): Commentary, Books I–IV*. Introductions; Commentary. Edited by W. Speed Hill. John E. Booty, Georges Edelen, Lee W. Gibbs, William P. Haugaard, and Arthur Stephen McGrade, contributing editors; with the assistance of Egil Grislis. 6 vols. Vol. 6 Part 2. Binghamton, NY: Medieval & Renaissance Texts & Studies, 1993.
———. *The Folger Library Edition of the Works of Richard Hooker (TFLE): Preface, Books I–IV*. Edited by Georges Edelen. W. Speed Hill, gen. ed. 6 vols. Vol. 1 Cambridge, MA: Belknap, 1977.
———. *The Folger Library Edition of the Works of Richard Hooker(TFLE): Preface, Book V*. Edited by Georges Edelen. W. Speed Hill, gen.ed. 6 vols. Vol. 2 Cambridge, MA: Belknap, 1977.
Hopkins, Luke. "Cyprian of Carthage and the Australian Anglican Episcopate." PhD diss, Melbourne: University of Divinity, 2020. https://repository.divinity.edu.au/4361/.
Inter-Anglican Theological and Doctrinal Commission. *Summary Argument from the IATDC's Communion Study*. http://www.anglicancommunion.org/ministry/theological/iatdc/docs/2006study.cfm.
Jeremias, Joachim. *New Testament Theology*. The New Testament Library. London: SCM, 1971.

Jones, Serene. *Trauma and Grace: Theology in a Ruptured World*. 2nd ed. Louisville: Westminster John Knox 2019.
Karris, Robert J., Helmut Koester, Eduard Lohse, and William R. Poehlmann. *Colossians and Philemon: A Commentary on the Epistles to the Colossians and to Philemon*. Translated by William R. Poehlmann and Robert J. Karris. Edited by Helmut Koester. Philadelphia: Fortress, 1971.
Kasemann, Ernst. *Essays on New Testament Themes*. London: SCM, 1964.
Kaye, Bruce Norman. *Conflict and the Practice of Christian Faith: The Anglican Experiment*. Eugene, OR: Cascade, 2009.
———. *Reinventing Anglicanism: A Vision of Confidence, Community and Engagement in Anglican Christianity*. Adelaide: Openbook, 2003.
———. *The Rise and Fall of the English Christendom: Theocracy, Christology, Order, and Power*. 1st ed. London: Routledge, 2017.
Kearsley, Roy. *Church, Community and Power*. Farnham, England: Ashgate, 2008.
Keenan, Marie. *Child Sexual Abuse and the Catholic Church: Gender, Power, and Organizational Culture*. Oxford: Oxford University Press, 2013.
Kotter, John P., and James L. Heskett. *Corporate Culture and Performance*. New York: Maxwell Macmillan, 1992.
Küng, Hans. *The Church*. London: Burns & Oates, 1967.
Lakeland, Paul. *Catholicism at the Crossroads: How the Laity Can Save the Church*. 1st ed. New York: Continuum, 2007.
The Lambeth Commission on Communion. *The Windsor Report*. 2004. https://www.anglicancommunion.org/media/68225/windsor2004full.pdf
Lathrop, Gordon W. *Holy Ground: A Liturgical Cosmology*. Philadelphia: Fortress 2003.
———. *Holy People: A Liturgical Ecclesiology*. Minneapolis: Fortress, 1999.
Lawrence, Thomas B. "Power, Institutions and Organizations." In *The Sage Handbook of Organizational Institutionalism*, edited by Royston Greenwood, 170–97. Thousand Oaks, CA: SAGE, 2017.
Lederach, John Paul. *Building Peace: Sustainable Reconciliation in Divided Societies*. Washington, DC: United States Institute of Peace Press, 1997.
———. *The Moral Imagination: The Art and Soul of Building Peace*. Oxford: Oxford University Press, 2005.
Lindberg, Tod. *The Political Teachings of Jesus*. 1st ed. New York: HC/Harper-Collins, 2007.
Littlejohn, W. Bradford. *The Peril and Promise of Christian Liberty: Richard Hooker, the Puritans, and Protestant Political Theology*. Emory University Studies in Law and Religion. Grand Rapids: Eerdmans, 2017.
Loisy, Alfred. *L'éVangile Et L'éGlise*. Paris: A. Picard et fils, 1902.
Lossky, Vladimir. *The Mystical Theology of the Eastern Church*. Crestwood, NY: St. Vladimir's Seminary Press, 1976.
Luhmann, Niklas. *A Systems Theory of Religion*. Translated by David A. Brenner & Adrian Hermann. Stanford, CA: Stanford University Press, 2013.
———. *Trust and Power*. Malden, MA: Polity, 2017.
Lutheran-Roman Catholic Commission on Unity. *The Apostolicity of the Church : Study Document of the Lutheran-Roman Catholic Commission on Unity*. Minneapolis: Lutheran University Press, 2006.
Mackay, Hugh. *Reinventing Australia: The Mind and Mood of Australia in the 90s*. Pymble, NSW: Angus & Robertson, 1993.

McCann, Joseph F. *Church and Organization: A Sociological and Theological Inquiry.* Scranton, PA: University of Scranton Press, 1993.
McCarthy, Michael Cornelius. "An Ecclesiology of Groaning: Augustine, the Psalms, and the Making of Church." *Theological Studies* 66.1 (2005) 23–48.
McConville, J. G. *God and Earthly Power: An Old Testament Political Theology, Genesis-Kings.* Library of Hebrew Bible/Old Testament Studies. London: T & T Clark, 2008.
McGrath, Alister E. *Christian Theology: An Introduction.* 25th Anniversary 6th ed. Chichester, West Sussex: Blackwell, 2017.
McLean, A. J. *Leadership and Cultural Webs in Organisations: Weavers' Tales.* Bingley, UK: Emerald, 2013.
Meeks, Wayne. *The First Urban Christians: The Social World of the Apostle Paul.* New Haven: Yale University Press, 1983.
Mickelsen, Alvera. *Women, Authority & the Bible.* Downers Grove, IL: InterVarsity, 1986.
Miller, Seumas. *The Moral Foundations of Social Institutions: A Philosophical Study.* Cambridge: Cambridge University Press, 2010.
Moloney, Francis J. *The Gospel of Mark: A Commentary.* Peabody, MA: Hendrickson, 2002.
Moltmann, Jürgen. *The Church in the Power of the Spirit: A Contribution to Messianic Ecclesiology.* London: SCM, 1977.
———. *The Power of the Powerless.* 1st US ed. San Francisco: Harper & Row, 1983.
———. *The Trinity and the Kingdom: The Doctrine of God.* Minneapolis: Fortress, 1993.
Morris, Leon. *The Gospel According to John.* Grand Rapids: Eerdmans, 1971.
Moule, C. F. D. *The Epistles of Paul the Apostle to the Colossians and to Philemon.* Cambridge: Cambridge University Press, 1957.
Newman, John Henry. *Tracts for the Times, Tract 1.* London: J. G. & F. Rivington, 1838.
North, Douglass C. *Institutions, Institutional Change, and Economic Performance.* Cambridge: Cambridge University Press, 1990.
O'Brien, Peter T. "Principalities and Powers: Opponents of the Church." In *Biblical Interpretation and the Church,* edited by D. A. Carson, 110–50. Exeter: Paternoster, 1984.
O'Hannay, James. *The Spirit and Origin of Christian Monasticism.* London: Methuen & Co., 1903.
O'Donovan, Oliver, and Joan Lockwood O'Donovan. *From Irenaeus to Grotius: A Sourcebook in Christian Political Thought, 100–1625.* Grand Rapids: Eerdmans, 1999.
Olsson, Trevor, and Donna Chung. *Report of the Board of Inquiry into the Handling of Claims of Sexual Abuse and Misconduct within the Anglican Diocese of Adelaide.* Adelaide: Anglican Diocese of Adelaide, 2004.
Painter, John. *Mark's Gospel: Worlds in Conflict.* New Testament Readings. London: Routledge, 1997.
Parkinson, Patrick. *Child Sexual Abuse and the Churches.* London: Hodder & Stoughton, 1997.
Parsons, Talcott, and Leon H. Mayhew. *Talcott Parsons on Institutions and Social Evolution: Selected Writings.* Chicago: University of Chicago Press, 1982.
Percy, Martyn. *Christ and Culture.* London: Canterbury Press, 2010.
———. *Clergy: The Origin of Species.* London: Continuum, 2006.
———. "Emergent Archiepiscopal Leadership Within the Anglican Communion." *Journal of Anglican Studies* 14.1 (2016) 46–70.
———. *Engaging with Contemporary Culture: Christianity, Theology and the Concrete Church.* London: Routledge, 2016.

———. *The Future Shapes of Anglicanism: Currents, Contours, Charts.* London: Routledge, 2016.
———. *Power and Christian Theology.* London: Continuum, 2006.
———. *Power and the Church: Ecclesiology in an Age of Transition.* London: Cassell, 1998.
Percy, Martyn, et al. *Engaging with Contemporary Culture: Christianity, Theology and the Concrete Church.* Abingdon: Taylor & Francis, 2005.
Pickard, Stephen. *Seeking the Church: An Introduction to Ecclesiology.* London: SCM, 2012.
———. *Theological Foundations for Collaborative Ministry.* Farnham: Ashgate, 2009.
Pickard, Stephen, and Jeffrey Driver. "'Re-Placing' Bishops: An Ecumenical and Trinitarian Approach to Episcopacy." *St Mark's Review* 169 (1997) 23–28.
Pitts, Jamie. *Principalities and Powers: Revising John Howard Yoder's Sociological Theology.* Cambridge: Lutterworth, 2014.
Ployd, Adam. *Augustine, the Trinity, and the Church: A Reading of the Anti-Donatist Sermons.* Oxford Studies in Historical Theology. London: Oxford University Press, 2015.
Rad, Gerhard von. *Deuteronomy: A Commentary.* London: SCM, 1973.
Radner, Ephraim. *The End of the Church: A Pneumatology of Christian Division in the West.* Cambridge: Eerdmans, 1998.
——— *Hope among the Fragments: The Broken Church and its Engagement of Scripture.* Grand Rapids: Brazos, 2004.
Radner, Ephraim, and Philip Turner. *The Fate of Communion: The Agony of Anglicanism and the Future of a Global Church.* Grand Rapids: Eerdmans, 2006.
Rambo, Shelly. *Spirit and Trauma: A Theology of Remaining.* 1st ed. Louisville: Westminster John Knox, 2010.
Renzetti, Claire M. *Clergy Sexual Abuse: Social Science Perspectives.* Boston: Northeastern, 2013.
Richardson, Cyril Charles. *Early Christian Fathers.* The Library of Christian Classics. New York: Macmillan, 1970.
Richardson, D., and Alan Cadwallader, eds. *Episcopacy: Views from the Antipodes.* Adelaide: Anglican Board of Christian Education, 1994.
Roberts, Richard H. "Lord, Bondsman and Churchman: Identity, Integrity and Power in Anglicanism." In *On Being the Church: Essays on the Christian Community,* edited by Colin Gunton and Daniel Hardy, 156–224. Edinburgh: T & T Clark, 1989.
Sappington, Thomas J. *Revelation and Redemption at Colossae.* London: Bloomsbury, 1991.
Schaff, Philip. *Nicene and Post-Nicene Fathers.* Christian Classics Ethereal Library, 2010. http://www.newadvent.org/fathers/160323.htm.
Schein, Edgar H. *Organizational Culture and Leadership.* 2nd ed. San Francisco: Jossey-Bass, 1992.
Secor, Philip Bruce. *Richard Hooker: Prophet of Anglicanism.* Tunbridge Wells: Burns & Oates, 1999.
Smith, Gordon T. *Institutional Intelligence: How to Build an Effective Organization.* Downers Grove, IL: InterVarsity, 2017.
Stark, Rodney. *The Rise of Christianity: A Sociologist Reconsiders History.* Princeton: Princeton University Press, 1996.
Stead, Michael. "To 'Rule Over' and 'Subdue' the Creation." https://anglican.org.au/wp-content/uploads/2019/05/To-Rule-and-To-Subdue-in-Genesis-1-Michael-Stead.pdf.

Steed, Lyndall G., and Robyn Downing. "Vicarious Traumatisation Amongst Psychologists and Professional Counsellors Working in the Field of Sexual Abuse/Assault." *Australasian Journal of Disaster and Trauma Studies* 2 (1998) n.p.

Stevenson, James. *A New Eusebius: Documents Illustrative of the History of the Church to A.D. 337*. London: SPCK, 1974.

Sullivan, Francis A. *From Apostles to Bishops: The Development of the Episcopacy in the Early Church*. New York: Newman, 2001.

Sykes, Stephen. *The Integrity of Anglicanism*. London: Mowbrays, 1978.

———. *Power and Christian Theology*. London: Continuum, 2006.

Theissen, Gerd. *The Open Door: Variations on Biblical Themes*. London: SCM, 1991.

Tomlinson, Ian, and Martyn Percy. *Clergy, Culture and Ministry: The Dynamics of Roles and Relations in Church and Society*. London: SCM, 2017.

Turner, Jonathan H. *The Institutional Order: Economy, Kinship, Religion, Polity, Law, and Education in Evolutionary and Comparative Perspective*. New York: Longman, 1997.

Turner, Stuart W., et al. "The Therapeutic Environment and New Explorations in the Treatment of Posttraumatic Stress Disorder." In *Traumatic Stress: The Effects of Overwhelming Experience on Mind, Body, and Society*, edited by Bessell A. van der Kolk et al., 3–23. London: Guilford, 1996.

Lutheran-Roman Catholic Commission on Unity. *The Apostolicity of the Church: Study Document of the Lutheran-Roman Catholic Commission on Unity*. Minneapolis: Lutheran University Press, 2006.

Van der Kolk, Bessell A. "The Black Hole of Trauma." In *Traumatic Stress: The Effects of Overwhelming Experience on Mind, Body, and Society*, edited by Bessell A. van der Kolk et al., 3–23. London: Guilford, 1996.

———. *The Body Keeps the Score: Mind, Brain and Body in the Transformation of Trauma*. London: Penguin, 2015.

Van der Kolk, Bessel A., et al. *Traumatic Stress: The Effects of Overwhelming Experience on Mind, Body, and Society*. London: Guilford, 1996.

Vergara, Lius Garrido. "Elites, Political Elites and Social Change in Modern Societies." *Revista de Sociologa* 28 (2013) 31–49.

Volf, Miroslav. *After Our Likeness: The Church as the Image of the Trinity*. Sacra Doctrina. Grand Rapids: Eerdmans, 1998.

———. *The End of Memory: Remembering Rightly in a Violent World*. Grand Rapids: Eerdmans, 2006.

Weber, Max. *Economy and Society: An Outline of Interpretive Sociology*, vol. 1. Edited by Guenther Roth and Claus Wittich. 2 vols. Berkeley: University of California Press, 1978.

Weeden, Theodore J. *Mark: Traditions in Conflict*. Philadelphia: Fortress, 1971.

Williams, Rowan. *Anglican Identities*. London: Darton, Longman & Todd, 2004.

———. "Hooker the Theologian." *Journal of Anglican Studies* 1.1 (2003) 104–16.

———. *On Christian Theology*. Oxford: Blackwell, 2000.

———. *Resurrection: Interpreting the Easter Gospel*. Rev. ed. London: Darton, Longman & Todd, 2002.

———. *The Truce of God*. London: Collins, in association with Faith Press, 1983.

Wilson, Bryan R. *Religion in Sociological Perspective*. Oxford: Oxford University Press, 1982.

Wilson, George B. *Clericalism: The Death of Priesthood*. Collegeville, MN: Liturgical, 2008.

Wink, Walter. *Engaging the Powers: Discernment and Resistance in a World of Domination*. Minneapolis: Fortress, 1992.

———. *Naming the Powers: The Language of Power in the New Testament*. Philadelphia: Fortress, 1984.

———. *The Powers That Be: Theology for a New Millennium*. 1st ed. New York: Doubleday, 1998.

———. *Unmasking the Powers: The Invisible Forces That Determine Human Existence*. Philadelphia: Fortress, 1986.

———. *When the Powers Fall: Reconciliation in the Healing of Nations*. Minneapolis: Fortress, 1998.

Wollebaek, Dag. "Age, Size and Change in Local Voluntary Associations." In *Acta Sociologica* 52.4 (2009) 365–84.

Wright, N. T. *How God Became King: The Forgotten Story of the Gospels*. 1st. ed. New York: HarperOne, 2012.

———. *Jesus and the Victory of God*. Christian Origins and the Question of God. 1st North American ed. Minneapolis: Fortress, 1996.

———. *The Contemporary Quest for Jesus*. Minneapolis: Fortress, 2002.

Wuthnow, Robert. *America and the Challenges of Religious Diversity*. Princeton: Princeton University Press, 2005.

Yoder, John Howard. *The Politics of Jesus: Vicit Agnus Noster*. Grand Rapids: Eerdmans, 1972.

INDEX

Aaronic priesthood, 52
absolutism, 65
abuse
    cover-up of, 25, 26, 67–69, 78, 129, 131, 133
    cultural symbols, 95–96
    idealizing the church, 131–32
    of power, 22–25, 26, 35, 61, 76, 101–2, 101n13
    reification, 70
    responses to, 3, 77–78, 99, 112–13, 129–31
    Royal Commission on, 1n1, 2–3, 2n4, 8–10, 10n23, 23, 26, 26n34, 78, 90n43, 92, 99–101, 102, 112, 116
    selfhood and integration, 103
    sexual abuse, 2n3, 2n4, 7, 9, 26, 77–78, 89, 89n42, 99–100, 108, 112, 117
    shame and trauma, 134–35
    survivors of, 3, 71, 112, 117, 134, 134n11, 136–40
access to greater meaning, 15, 83
accountability, 4, 21, 23, 25, 69, 72, 96, 107, 117, 123, 129, 133–34, 134n11
Acts, 41, 48–49, 54
actual and ideal, 33–35, 68–69, 69n42, 132
adamah, 30
Adelaide, Australia, 77, 117, 134n11, 136–37
administrative functions of the church, 67, 71, 118–20, 123

adult maturity, 111–12
alliance of church and empire, 58–61
ambiguity, 36, 94
An Admonition to Parliament, 79–80
angels, 44
Anglican Church, 12
    apostolic succession, 103–7
    clericalism, 100, 109–10
    debate about Anglican orders, 105n24
    ecclesiology, 68
    Hooker and the Puritans, 79–83
    House of Bishops, 133n10
    idealizing of church, 72
    institutional governance and management, 25, 116–18
    method of consensual working, 133
    model of episcopacy, 121–24
    modern liturgical movement, 76
    royal commission, 2, 2n5, 9, 10n23, 26n34
    Trinity Sunday worship, 73–74, 89–92
    Weber's Patrimonial Maintenance, 109n32
Anglican Diocese of Adelaide, 77, 117
AnglicareSA, 117
animals, 31n8
anti-ritualism, 85
Anzac Day, 77–78
apostolicity, 105, 105n22, 126
apostolic succession, 103–7
apprenticeship system, 98
Arbuckle, Gerald, 26, 67, 67n40, 99n3
Archbishops' Council, 119

INDEX

architecture, 60, 71, 74–75, 78, 90n43
Aristotelian metaphysics, 103
Assyria, 29
Athanasius of Alexandria, 104
Augustine, 56–57, 61–62, 63, 94
Australia, 1–2, 2n3, 7, 7n17, 10n23, 77, 84, 87n35, 90–92, 93n47, 99n4, 108n30, 109–10, 109n33, 116–18, 118n6, 122n15, 123n20, 124n21, 124n24, 133n10. See also *A Prayer Book for Australia*; Royal Commission into Institutional Responses to Child Sexual Abuse
Australian Defence Force and Police, 8n17
authenticity, 38, 129
authorities, 5, 29, 41, 44, 48–50, 64, 66n35, 66n36, 75, 86, 106, 109n32, 133–34
autocracy, 115
Avis, Paul, 64n29

Babylon, 29–33, 29n1, 30n5, 116
baptism, 70, 88, 94, 103
basic modules of Christianity, Brown, 58
Bathsheba, 34–35
Battle of Milvian Bridge, 58
belonging, 17, 40, 126, 132
Berger, Peter L., 70n46
Berkhof, Hendrikus, 41, 43
bishops
  in Anglican Communion, 133, 133n10
  apostolic succession, 104–6, 105n22, 106n26
  cathedrals, 92
  Church of England, 118–19
  and clericalism, 100, 107–9
  consecration, 119–20
  under Constantine, 58–60, 122n14
  cultural change, 116–18, 127n28
  Irenaeus on, 122n16
  Lambeth Conference of 2008, 136–40
  Ordination of Bishops, 123n19
  ordination of women, 90n43
  practices that reinforce clericalism, 111n37
  reconfiguring of dioceses, 120–25
  re-placing bishops, 127
  re-placing symbols, 93
  Roman world, 56–57
  as stewards of culture, 125–26
  Trinity Sunday worship, 73–75, 89–90
Black Rock mural, 7, 7n16
body language, 88–92
Boniface VIII (pope), 63
Book of Common Prayer, 130
Brent, Alan, 121
Brett, Mark, 33
British Empire, 109n32, 122
Brown, Peter, 58
Brunner, Emil, 13, 18, 21–22
bushfires, 7n17

Callistus, 56, 56n10
Calvin, John, 63
Cartwright, Thomas, 79
cathedrals, 73–74, 89–93
Catholic Emancipation Act 1829, 106n25
catholicity, 56–57, 126
ceremonies, 76, 77–83, 86–87, 90–91
change. See cultural change
channels, 23–24n28
charismatic church, 13, 40, 40n24
children, 2–3, 7, 9, 10n23, 15, 99–100, 113, 116, 137
Christian gentry in Asia Minor, 59n16
Christianity, basic modules of, 58
Christianity in the Roman Empire, 58n14, 58n16, 61
church, 1–4, 7–11
  apostolic succession, 103–7
  church and state, 63–65, 82
  church buildings, 58, 75–76, 128
  church leaders, 60, 71, 95, 99–100
  church visible, 20
  cultural change, 84–85, 112–13, 134–35
  and empire, 61–63
  as herald, 23
  Hooker's principles, 82–83

152

INDEX

idealizing, 66–69
institutional model of, 19
institutional workings of the world, 15–19
ongoing change, 116–18
and ordination, 102–3
paradox in self-understanding, 65
reconfiguring of dioceses, 120–25
re-receiving symbols, 95–96
Roman world, 57–61
searching for, 128–31
as self-sufficient and unchanging, 66, 105
wheat and weeds parable, 56–57
See also bishops; clergy; clericalism
Church Commission, 119
Church of England, 79, 83, 105, 106n25, 118–19
cities, 32, 48, 60, 62, 139–40, 523
Clement of Rome, 104
clergy, 59, 68, 71, 101, 107–9, 109n31, 109n32, 109n33, 111, 111n37, 123, 127n28, 133
clericalism, 9, 92, 97–113
   apostolic succession, 103–7
   clerical monotheism, 40n24
   cultural and symbolic props of, 107–11
   and laity, 111–12
   ordination and ontology, 102–3
   overdevelopment of, 21
   slow response to abuse, 112–13
   vocational affirmation, 101–2
closed religious order, 76
codices, 58
Collins, John, 39
colonial expansion, 91n44, 122
Colossae, 44
Commodus (emperor), 58n16
commonality, 10n23, 83, 87–88, 109
common good, 5, 8, 98
Commonwealth and Cromwellian eras in English history, 65n34
communion, 68
community
   community-creating, 47–50
   community distrust, 4, 6
   Cyprianic model, 121–23

and development of institutional forms, 13–14, 19–23
and dominion, 31
and Jesus, 53
ownership and autonomy, 115–16
place as a marker of, 122n15
relationality of episcopacy, 127
of saints, 57
secondary trauma, 134, 137–38
conciliarism, 65, 82, 86, 133
confer, 38–39, 39n21
conformists, 64, 82–83
congruity, 77, 82, 87, 90
consecration, 119–20, 126
consensual working, 133
consensus, 22, 30–31, 133n9
Constantine, 57–61, 58n13, 59n17, 122, 122n14
Constantinople, 60
contemporary organizational models, 120
contextual diversity, 83
continuity, 16, 20, 53–54, 94, 104–5, 126
control, 32
conversion, 48, 58, 59n17, 86
cooperation, 21
Corinth, 55, 102n14, 104
cosmologies, 29–33, 74–75, 86, 92, 95
Council of Bishops at Elvira, 59n16
Council of Nicaea, 59–60
covenant, 33, 38–39, 39n21
cover-up of abuse, 25, 26, 67–69, 78, 129, 131, 133
COVID-19 pandemic, 7, 7n17, 8, 77–78, 79n10, 84n27, 108n30, 124–25, 124n23, 128–29
creation myths, 29–32, 29n1, 30–31nn5–7
creation order, 90n43
creeping infallibility, 67
cultural change, 10, 110–13, 126n28, 134–35, 140
cultural context, 29, 83, 85, 90–95, 124
cultural symbols, 92, 95, 108n30
culture, bishops as stewards of, 117, 125–26
culture based distrust, 4

153

cynicism, 4, 130, 138
Cyprianic model, 121–23, 127, 133

Dardanelles, 77
dark shadow, 10, 18
David, 34–35, 34–35n13, 132n6
Dawson, Brigitte, 7n16
defensive responses to abuse, 3, 77–78, 129–31
deification, 33. *See also* idealization of the church
Dei Filius, 66, 66n35
delineation of the canon of Scripture, 104
democracy, 6, 24
denial of power, 28, 39, 50
denominational pluralism, 106
Deuteronomic history, 33, 33n10, 52
diakonein, 39
diaspora, 116
differentials in power, 13, 22
digital communication, 79, 84n27, 88, 128
diocesan bishops, 92, 110n34, 111n37, 117, 119, 127n28, 133n10
diocesan council, 117, 137–38
diocesan synod, 133, 133n9, 134n11
dioceses, 59, 107, 117–23, 123n20, 124n21, 127, 127n28, 133, 136–38
Diocletian, 57
The Disarming Child (Moltmann), 45
disciples, 16, 19, 36–39, 37n20, 45, 48
disillusionment, 4
dissent, 24, 61, 65, 67n40, 70, 71, 106, 134
distortion(s), 13, 18, 21–22, 25–26, 28, 32–33, 35, 38, 43–45, 44n32, 46, 49–50, 61, 69, 102, 107, 130
distribution of power, 13, 22–23
distribution of wealth, 15
distrust, 4, 8–11
diversity, 24, 61, 68, 74, 83, 87, 95
Doctrine Commission of the Anglican Church of Australia, 103n17
domination, 29–33, 30n6, 34, 43, 89
dominion, 29–32, 31n8, 32n9
Donatists, 56–57

Douglas, Mary, 67n40, 85–87, 85n28, 88, 91
Dulles, Avery, 18–23, 20n17, 20n19, 26–27n36, 67
Durkheim, Emile, 34, 79, 85–86
dynastic succession, 35

earthly power, 34–35, 46
earthly structures, 55, 57, 61–62, 65, 67–69, 71
Easter, 47–49, 50n42, 54, 130–31, 131n5, 135
ecclesia, 13, 17n8, 22
ecclesiology, 10–14, 18, 106, 132–34
  ecclesial idealism, 56, 68
  ecclesial identity, 126
  ecclesiological framework, 85
  idealizing the church, 66–69
  institutional model, 20–22
  and power, 60–61
  servant church, 38
  wheat and weeds, 56–57
  working ecclesiology, 110–11
economic systems, 6
ecumenical councils, 133
Edict of Milan, 59
edification, 82–83
elites, 21, 98–101, 108, 111
Elohim/Yahweh, 29–30
Emmaus, 138–40
Engaging the Powers (Wink), 41
England, 122
English Reformation, 64, 133, 133n8
Enlightenment, 5, 84n27
Ephesians, 44
episcopacy, 121, 123, 125, 127, 133
episcopal ministry, 119, 120–21, 126–27
episcopal succession, 105
equality, 23, 32, 63, 95
Erastian paradigm, 106
eschatological fulfillment, 43, 57, 67–68
eschatology, 54–55
Esler, Philip Francis, 54n5
Essenes in Palestine, 132
Eucharist, 49n42, 85, 88, 94, 95, 103
Eucharistic Thanksgiving for Easter Day, 130–31, 131n5

INDEX

Europe, 41, 66, 87, 91n44, 109
Eusebius, 60
evil, 41, 43, 57, 62, 67
excommunication, 63
execution, 63
exodus, 114–16
Ezekiel, 52

faithfulness, 28, 34, 51, 95, 105, 105n22, 105n24
false developments, 13, 18, 22
family, 32
fellowship, 13, 55, 95
Final Report, Royal Commission into Institutional Responses to Child Sexual Abuse, 2–3, 9–10, 26n34, 116–17
First Letter to the Corinthians, 55
First Urban Christians (Meeks), 58n14
First Vatican Council, 66
five models of Dulles, 19–26
Forbes, Chris, 41
formalistic impersonality, 24–25
Foucault, Michael, 99n3
founding fathers, 93
frontline institutions, 7
fulfillment, 5, 18, 34, 53–55, 54nn4–5

Galatia, 43–44
Gallipoli, 77
garden of the ideal, 32–33
Gelasius (pope), 63
Genesis, 29–33, 29n1, 52, 90n43
getting over the institutional church, 25–27
Gibbons, Andrew, 8n17
Giddens, Anthony, 23
gift of order, 21
Gillard, Julia, 2
globalization, 124–25
Gnosticism, 103–4
God language, 94
god of heaven and a god of earth, 30n5
God's dominion, 29–35, 34n13. *See also* people of God; trinitarian ecclesiology
good and evil, 57

governance, 40–41, 63–64, 117–18, 133–34, 133n9
Granfield, Patrick, 66–67
great commission, 16–17

Habel, Norman, 31n7
Handy, Charles, 115
Hardy, Dan, 17
Heclo, Hugh, 1n1, 4–6, 5n8, 14n4, 84n27
Henn, William, 105
herald, model of church as, 19, 23
heresy, 13
Hezekiah, 35
hierarchy, 13, 21, 30–33, 63, 67, 74–76, 74n1, 82, 92, 95–96, 99
high-profile level, Maclean, 110, 112, 112n40, 126
Hillsong, 86n33, 124, 124n21
Hippolytus, 56
holiness, 28, 34, 55–56, 58, 65, 72, 92, 126
holy communion, 70
Holy Saturday, 135
Holy Trinity, 68–69, 74, 95
honor, 37–40
Hooker, Richard, 64–65, 71, 79–83, 85, 86–87, 90–92
Hopkins, Luke, 121, 125
Hosier Lane, 8n17
House of Bishops, 133
housing provisions for clergy, 109–10
human behavior, influences or constraints on, 1n1, 15
human body, 88–92
human city, 52
humanity, 5, 17, 30–31, 30n6, 62
human power system, 30–33, 35–36, 38, 41
human reason, 5, 63
human sociality, 13, 17, 33, 68

IATDC (Inter-Anglican Theological and Doctrinal Commission), 69n42
ideal and actual, 33–35, 68–69, 69n42, 132

155

INDEX

idealization of the church, 18, 23, 26, 40, 66–69, 71–72, 101, 129, 131–32
identity, 15–17, 29, 34, 76, 78–79, 106–7, 116, 122, 126
Ignatius of Antioch, 123
image of God, 30, 30n6
images, 18–19
imperial institutions, 57–61
imprisonment and trial of the apostles, 48
incarnation, 17, 45, 81, 109
inequalities, 22–23, 35
inevitable hierarchy, 13
Inquisition, 65
institutions, 1–3, 1n1, 12–27, 14n4, 22n25, 23, 28, 131–32
    biblical narrative, 51–53
    Constantine and imperial institutions, 57–61
    COVID-19 lockdowns, 7
    exceptions to distrust, 8–11
    getting over the institutional church, 25–26
    idealizing the church, 67–69
    institutionalism, 21–22
    institutional model of the church, 19–22
    institution-aversion, 4–6
    and monarchy, 34
    Pauline language, 42
    reifying church structures, 69–71
    secondary trauma, effects of, 134–35
    symbolism and ceremony, 76
Inter-Anglican Theological and Doctrinal Commission (IATDC), 69n42
international network churches, 124
intuition, 87, 91
Irenaeus, 104, 122, 122n16
Israel, 29, 33n10, 35, 38–39, 52–53, 54, 116

James, 37, 40
Jeremiah, 52
Jerusalem, 33n10, 40, 49, 52, 62, 116, 125, 132, 138–40
Jesus, 16–17, 21n20, 36–40, 37n20, 39n21, 46, 47–50, 48n40, 50n42, 52–55, 78n7, 94–96, 109–11, 116, 116n4, 138–40
Jethro, 115
Jewish Law, 44
Jewish rabbis, 53
John, 37, 40, 44, 46, 54, 134–35
Jordan, 125
Josiah, 35
Judah, 33n10, 35, 125

katakuriow, 39–40
Kaye, Bruce, 59n17, 123
Keenan, Mary, 103n18
kerygmatic, 23
kingdom, ideal of, 35
kingdom and glory, 37
kingdom of God, 17n8, 18, 26, 62, 96
kingdoms, doctrine of earthly and heavenly, 63, 65
kingship, 34–35, 52n1
kinship, 15, 32, 33
klaeros, 102
knowledge, 15, 22–23, 55, 84n27, 94, 97–99, 101, 104
knowledge elites, 98–99
koinonia (fellowship), 3, 13, 95. See also community
Küng, Hans, 10–11, 18

labor, 32
laikos, 102
laity, 21, 101, 106–7, 111–12, 123, 133
Lakeland, Paul, 111–12
Lambeth Conference of 2008, 136–40
language as symbol system, 93–94
language of prayer and worship, 130–31
laos, 102
Lateran Palace, 59
Lathrop, Gordon, 92n45
Lawes (Hooker), 81
Lawrence, Thomas B., 22n25
leadership
    apostolic succession, 103–7
    failures of, 2, 4
    institutionalism, 21

INDEX

Lathrop on, 92n45
leadership elites, 99–101
  legitimation to institutions, 25
  ordering of by Jesus, 39
  organization, 14
  Pauline churches, 40
  power differentials, 22
  reconfiguring of, 114–26
  reification, 70
  response to abuse, 78, 99
  vocational affirmation, 71
  Weber on, 109n32
  women in, 90n43
  See also bishops; power(s)
legitimizing of power, 15, 24–25, 31, 40, 47, 121
Lester, Alison, 17n10, 129n1
Levant, Brian, 17n10, 129n1
liberalism, 66, 105
Licinius, 59
liturgical movement, 75–76
liturgical reforms, 95–96
liturgy, 72, 74–76, 95–96
loud fences, 7
Luhman, Niklas, 24
Luke, 37, 37n20, 38–39, 48, 54, 139–40
Luther, Martin, 63–64

Mackay, Hugh, 84
Maclean, Adrian, 110–12, 112n40
making disciples, 16–17
Marcia, 58n16
Marcionites, 56
Mark, 36–40, 37n20
Mary Magdalene, 134–35
mashal, 32
materialism, 66, 105
Matthew, 16–17, 37, 53–54, 54n4
McCann, Joseph, 26, 34
McLean, A. J., 126
Meeks, Wayne, 58n14
Melbourne, Australia, 7, 7n16, 8n17, 124, 124n23
metanoia, 10, 86, 96, 108
ministry, 9, 17, 36, 37n20, 70, 103, 108–9, 119, 120–21, 125, 126, 127
Mintzberg, Henry, 115
missio Dei, 124

Models of the Church (Dulles), 18–23, 20n17, 20n19, 26–27n36, 67
Modernism, 5, 84n17
modern market, 6
modern political democracy, 6
modern social systems, 24
Moltmann, Jürgen, 13, 18, 21–22, 40n24, 45
monarchical episcopate, 40n24
monarchy, 33–34, 52–53, 64–65, 75, 92
monasticism, 57, 132
Montanists, 56
Moses, 52, 114–15, 125–26
Mount Nebo, 125
mundane power, 38
murals, 7, 7n16, 8n17
mystical church, 64
mystical communion, 19, 21
mystical identity, 71

Naming the Powers (Wink), 41–42
Nathan, 34–35, 34n13, 132n6
national monuments and statues, 93
national redress scheme, 10n23
"A National Tragedy," 2–3
nations, 32, 34–35, 51–52, 71, 132
natural law, 63
Natural Symbols (Douglas), 88
Nazi Germany, 41, 43
negative aspects to institutional life, 24, 99
new exodus, 116
Newman, John Henry, 106, 106n26
New Testament, 18, 36, 40, 43–44, 53–54, 99n5, 102, 102n14, 104, 130
New Zealand, 77
non-zero game, 24
North Africa, 56–57
Novationism, 56

Old Adam, 63
On the City of God against the Pagans (Augustine), 61–62
oppression, 33–35, 93, 108n30
ordained ministry, 100–101, 103, 108

157

order and structure, 20–22, 30–32, 39, 42–43, 43n31, 70, 75–76, 88, 90n43, 100, 114–16, 121, 122, 122n15, 125, 131–34. *See also* hierarchy; institutions
ordinals, 100–101, 125, 126n28
ordination, 68, 90n43, 101–3, 103n18, 105n24, 106, 106n26
Ordination of Bishops, 123n19
organizational authority, Weber, 109n32
organizational culture, 10, 110–12, 110n36, 126
organizational shifts, 13
organizations, 1n1, 8n17, 14–17, 14n4, 24–25, 42n29, 114–15, 121. *See also* institutions
Orthodox Church, 58n13, 105, 123
overseer, 125
Oxford Movement, 106

papal power, 63, 133
Papua New Guinea, 91
parable of the wheat and weeds, 56–57
paradox in church self-understanding, 65
Parliament and Convocation, 133
Parsons, Talcott, 23–24, 23n28, 34
Passover, 53, 94, 116
Pastor Aeternus, 66, 66n35
Patrimonial Maintenance, 109n32
patronage systems of preindustrial Europe, 109
Paul (apostle), 40–45, 42n29, 47n38, 48–49, 54–55, 102n14, 129–30
Pell, George, 7, 7n15
penance, 56–57
people of God, 17, 28, 35, 38–39, 44, 49–50, 51, 52–53, 61, 83, 95, 99n5, 101, 105n24, 109, 116, 121, 123, 126, 130, 131–33
Percy, Martyn, 119–20, 134
perfect society, 21, 66–67
performance based distrust, 4
Pharisees, 45
Philistines, 34
Pickard, Stephen, 19, 21, 113n41, 119, 120–21, 134

Pilate, Pontius, 36, 45–46, 48
places of honor, 37, 40
politics/politicians, 6, 8n17, 22, 30, 30n5, 36, 39
possession of sacred Scriptures, 58
Power and Christian Theology (Sykes), 36
power(s), 28
  abuse of, 22–25, 26, 35, 61, 76, 101–2, 101n13
  Arbuckle on, 99n3
  church and empire, 59–61
  and clericalism, 107–12
  cosmology of, 29–33
  distortions of, 43–45, 47–50
  distribution of, 13
  earthly power, 34–35
  and elites, 98–99
  human divestment of, 45–47
  and institutionalism, 22–25, 23n28
  institutionality and, 131–33
  Mark passage, 36–40
  models of the church, 67
  New Testament language, 130
  of ordination, 106, 106n26
  Pauline language, 40–43
  polarities of, 36
  rigorist movement, 65
  sexual abuse, 89, 89n42
  size of organizations, 121
  and symbolism, 74–76
  two swords model, 63–64
  vocational affirmation, 71
A Prayer Book for Australia, 102n14, 123n19, 130–31
precedence, 74, 90, 91n44, 92, 96, 109
presbyters, 39, 123, 125
pre-Vatican II Church, 67, 67n40
priesthood, 13, 46, 52–53, 54, 100–101, 101n13, 103n18
primeval history in Genesis, 29, 29n1, 32–33, 90n43
principalities and powers, 42–43
processions, 90–91
proclamation, 23, 130n3, 131
professional elites, 108
Professional Standards Committee, 117
prophecy, 35, 52–53

INDEX

Protestants, 85
protest march, 76
public narrative, 78n7
Puritans, 64, 65, 65n34, 79–83, 86–87, 89, 132
purity, 55, 56–57, 88
Purity and Danger (Douglas), 88

radah (rule), 30, 30–31n7, 32
Rambo, Shelly, 130n3, 134
rationalism, 66
reconfiguring the diocese, 120–25
redress schemes, 3, 10n23
Reform Acts of 1832, 106n25
Reformation, 63–64, 82, 85, 86, 133, 133n8
reform(s), 53, 81, 82, 87, 95
reframing symbols, 89, 93–95
reification, 70–71, 70n45
religious institutions, 2, 9, 24, 70, 70n46, 76, 132
renewal. *See* reform(s)
repetition, 48
"'Re-Placing' Bishops" (Pickard and Driver), 120–21
re-placing symbols, 4, 93
re-receiving symbols, 4, 85, 95–96
residential institutions and schools, 2n5
Revelation to John, 44
rigorist movements, 56, 65, 132
rites, 85, 88–89, 95, 130
rituals, 70, 76, 77–79, 83, 85–87, 88
Roman Catholic Church, 2, 2n5, 9, 21, 59–60, 64n31, 66–67, 100, 103, 105–6, 106n25, 116
Roman Empire, 47, 47n38, 56, 58–59, 58n14, 61–62, 121–22
Romanticism, 5, 84n27
routinization of charisma, 100
Royal Commission into Institutional Responses to Child Sexual Abuse, 1n1, 2–3, 2n4, 8–10, 10n23, 23, 26, 26n34, 78, 90n43, 92, 99–101, 102, 112, 116

sacred priesthood, 13
sacrifice, 40, 46–47

salvation, 13, 17, 43, 64, 65n33, 130
Salvation Army workers during World War II, 8n18
same-sex unions, 68
Samuel, 34, 52n1
Saul, 34, 52n1
Schein, Edgar, 10, 126, 126–27n28
Schemata of the First Vatican Council, 66, 66n36
Scripture, 25, 26n36, 58, 63–64, 81–82, 94, 101, 104
secondary trauma, 134, 137–38, 137n3
secretariam, 61
Seeking the Church (Pickard), 113n41
self-giving of Christ, 47–49
selfhood and integration, 103
self-protection, 69, 107, 132
self-realization of the individual, 5
servant church, 19, 38
service, 36–39, 101–2, 109, 109n32
sexual abuse, 2n3, 2n4, 7, 9, 26, 77–78, 89, 89n42, 99–100, 108, 112, 117. *See also* cover-up of abuse; survivors of abuse
shame, 4, 89, 96, 108, 132, 134–35, 140
sign and narrative, 94
sign and signified, 82, 87, 89, 90–92. *See also* symbols
skill elites, 99
social change, 85–86
social dynamics, 70, 127
social elites, 97–98, 101, 108
social institutions, 15–16, 62, 100
sociality, 13, 17, 30, 33, 68
social relationships and boundaries, 88
social sciences, 10, 13, 70n46
social systems, 24
specialist knowledge, 22, 98, 101, 108
special language, 108
spiritual ministries, 67
stability, 16
Stark, Rodney, 58n14, 59n17
Stead, Michael, 31n7
stewardship, 30, 120, 126
street art, 7–8n17
subjection and exile, 29
submission to power, 40–42
Supremi Pastoris, 66, 67n37

INDEX

survivors of abuse, 3, 71, 112, 117, 134, 134n11, 136–40
Sykes, Stephen, 23, 36, 38, 74
symbols, 73–96
    body language, 88–92
    ceremony, crisis, and change, 77–78
    congruency and natural symbols, 86–88
    high-profile symbols, 112n40
    and Hooker, 79–83, 85, 86–87, 90–92
    low-profile symbols, 110n36, 130
    opposition, 77–78
    props of clericalism, 107–9
    reframing symbols, 93–95
    re-placing symbols, 93
    re-receiving symbols, 95–96
    ritualist belief, 85–86
synods, 105n22, 133–34, 133n9, 134n11
Synoptics, 37–38

table waiting, 39
teaching role, 21, 92, 122n16, 126
The Power of the Powerless (Moltmann), 45
Thomas Aquinas, 102–3
titles, 108–9, 111
toleration of dissent, 106
Tracts for the Times, Tract 1 (Newman), 106, 106n26
tradition, 16–17, 25, 36, 122–23
traditional biblical scholarship, 41
traditional churches, 4, 75–76, 90, 109n32, 121
trauma, 89, 130n3, 134–35, 136n1, 137–40, 137n3
Travers, Walter, 79, 79n11
trial of Jesus, 48n40
trinitarian ecclesiology, 68–69, 74, 95
Trinity Sunday worship, 73–74, 89–92
Troeltsch, Ernst, 54n5
Turner, Jonathan, 14–15
Turner, Melissa, 7n16

twelve tribes of Israel, 38, 53
two swords doctrine, 63–65
tyranny, 39, 65

unfolding, 17–18
unity, 60–61, 68–69, 104n21, 116, 125, 134n12
Unmasking the Powers (Wink), 41

values, 10, 15–16, 26, 26n36, 38, 84, 85
Vatican II, 66–68, 105n24
victim-sacrifice of Christ, 46, 48n40, 49
visibility, 20, 51, 64, 65–67, 69, 80, 104. See also symbols
Visigoths, 61
vocation, 26, 35, 44, 50, 51, 56, 67, 71, 92, 99n5, 101–3, 106, 108, 116, 120, 123n20, 132
vulnerable persons, 2, 4, 8–9, 33, 78n7, 89

Weber, Max, 24–25, 34, 100, 109n32
Weeden, Theodore, 37n20
Western churches, 102, 133
Western society and consciousness, 4–6, 8, 84n27
whistle-blowers, 26, 26n34
white coat syndrome, 97–98, 107, 108n30
Williams, Rowan, 48n40, 49–50n42, 81
will to power, 38–39, 69
Windsor Report, 68
Wink, Walter, 41–43, 42n29
wisdom of God, 44–45, 50
woman, 31–32, 32n9
working culture, 107–11
world powers, Pauline, 41
worldview, change of, 10, 31, 86
World War 1, 41, 77, 77n5
Yankelovich, Daniel, 5n8

Yoder, John H., 43

zero-sum game, 24
Zeus, 115, 115n2

www.ingramcontent.com/pod-product-compliance
Lightning Source LLC
Chambersburg PA
CBHW030858170426
43193CB00009BA/648